Omer

A Counting

OMER
A Counting

❧ Rabbi Karyn D. Kedar

INTRODUCTION BY

Rabbi A. Brian Stoller

CENTRAL CONFERENCE OF AMERICAN RABBIS

Editorial Advisory Group

Rabbi Jeff Goldwasser

Rabbi Josee Hudson

Rabbi Darah Lerner

Rabbi Andrew Vogel

Rabbi Hara E. Person, Publisher and Director, CCAR Press

Rabbi Steven A. Fox, Chief Executive, Central Conference of
American Rabbis

Library of Congress Cataloging-in-Publication Data

Kedar, Karyn D., 1957- author.
Omer : a counting / Rabbi Karyn D. Kedar ; introduction by Rabbi A. Brian Stoller.
   pages cm
ISBN 978-0-88123-219-6 (pbk. : alk. paper)
1. Sefirah period. 2. Reform Judaism--Customs and practices. I. Title.

BM695.S4K43 2014
296.4'39--dc23

2014003275)

10 9 8 7 6 5 4 3 2 1

CCAR Press, 355 Lexington Avenue, New York, NY 10017
(212) 972-3636
ccarpress.org

To Chime

It was in the garden at dusk,
and the wind whispered, or maybe sighed
and I heard the sound of God.

Contents

Acknowledgments

Thank you:

To the people of Congregation B'nai Jehoshua Beth Elohim, who simply asked, all the time, so are you writing another book?

To Rabbi Hara Person, the Publisher and Director of CCAR Press, whose strength, wisdom, and diligence guide us, guide me. Thanks also to the CCAR staff who helped make this book happen: Rabbi Steven A. Fox, Deborah Smilow, Ortal Bensky, Cori Carl, and Dan Medwin, as well as rabbinic interns Daniel Kirzane, Adena Kemper, and Liz Piper-Goldberg.

To the beautiful teenagers who helped with citations, Sara Splansky, Maren Gelfond, and Rachel Kunz. To Teri Costello, whose sharp eye read and reread the manuscript. To Hilary Larson, who sees all things as lovely. To Arna Yastrow, my patient, wise friend.

To my parents, Norman and Lynore Schwartz, who always believed in the extraordinary. To my husband, Ezra, and our children and grandchildren, who make me exquisitely ordinary.

Introduction

RABBI A. BRIAN STOLLER

*From the day on which you bring the omer of elevation offering—
the day after the Sabbath—you shall count off seven weeks. They must
be complete: you must count until the day after the seventh week—
fifty days; then you shall bring an offering of new grain to Adonai.*
LEVITICUS 23:15–16

*Just as all the crops are ripening during these days [of counting],
so too is the life of man revealed [during this time]. For all of it is but an
allusion to the way of the inner life.* S'FAT EMET

*No fraction of time . . . should slip through the fingers, left unex-
ploited; for eternity may depend upon the brief moment.*
RABBI JOSEPH SOLOVEITCHIK

Counting the Omer,[1] the traditional practice of counting the forty-nine days between Passover and Shavuot, is making a comeback in Reform Judaism. Once virtually ignored as an ancient custom that had lost its religious significance, *S'firat HaOmer* (as it is known in Hebrew) is now increasingly regarded among Reform Jews as a meaningful way to

---

1 On the *halachot* of *S'firat HaOmer*, see Leviticus 23:9–21; *Mishneh Torah, Hilchot T'midim uMusafim* 7:3–25; *Sefer HaChinuch*, commandments 302–306 (*Parashat Emor*); and *Shul-chan Aruch, Orach Chayim* 489:1. The requirements for Counting the Omer outlined in this introduction are drawn from these sources, unless otherwise noted.

mark time, express gratitude, refocus priorities, and contemplate deeply the meaning and purpose of our existence.

Rabbi Karyn D. Kedar, one of the Reform Movement's most inspiring authors and composers of creative liturgy, introduced the practice to her community in Deerfield, Illinois, several years ago by e-mailing her congregants a short reading or prayer each day of the Omer and inviting them to reflect on it. Their responses were thoughtful and deeply emotional. Congregants wrote heartfelt notes about how the daily messages had touched their lives and provided a spark of inspiration in the middle of their busy days, they circulated the e-mails to their friends and family, and soon an entire congregation of Reform Jews who previously had never heard of Counting the Omer came to regard it as one of the most meaningful spiritual events of the year.

This book, which is a continuation of Rabbi Kedar's initial project, aims to help the broader Reform community similarly experience the power of *S'firat HaOmer*. In some sense it is like a prayer book: just as a prayer book gives us the vocabulary to pray, this book gives us a vocabulary to count the Omer through daily meditation on contemporary poetry and prose, both Jewish and secular. Before we can begin counting the days and contemplating these texts, however, we need to understand the basics of *S'firat HaOmer* and some of the key spiritual insights that emerge from Jewish interpretation of this practice.

Spiritual Dimensions of *S'firat HaOmer*

The Nature and Purpose of Wealth

The period from the second day of Passover to Shavuot coincides with the spring harvest in *Eretz Yisrael* (the Land of Israel). The rituals prescribed in the Torah structure the time and activity of this season so as to elevate consciousness of and inspire gratitude for God's role as the source of the bounty. To sanctify the harvest's beginning, the biblical Jew was commanded to bring to the Jerusalem Temple an omer offering of barley, the first fruit to ripen during the season. Giving God the first and best of the new crop, in a measure amounting to "sufficient food for a person for one day,"[2] meant putting God before one's own personal needs and satisfaction. Indeed, a person was not permitted to eat anything from the harvest until he had brought the omer offering—an acknowledgment that, without God, his abundance and sustenance would not be possible. The counting of the Omer commenced immediately thereafter, numbering the days until Shavuot, which ritually marked the end of the harvest season.

Though most Reform Jews today (especially outside *Eretz Yisrael*) do not live in farming societies, these agricultural themes are eminently relevant to modern Jewish life. Broadly understood, the "harvest season" is when we reap the fruits of our labors, whether on the farm, in commerce, or wherever we earn our livelihood. This is the time when instinct and societal norms tell us finally to relax and enjoy the abundance we have sown. But as Rabbi Samson Raphael Hirsch points out, this moment when others stop counting is precisely the moment when Jews *begin* to count,[3] affirming the connection between our God-given freedom to produce (symbolized in Passover) and our responsibility to dedicate what we reap to the service of God (embodied in Shavuot). *S'firat HaOmer* thus teaches us that wealth is not an end unto itself, but rather, as Hirsch writes, that "material prosperity has meaning only insofar as it helps attain and maintain right and morality."[4] The act of

---

2 Rabbi Samson Raphael Hirsch, comment to Leviticus 23:10, in *The Hirsch Chumash: Sefer Vayikra—Part 2*, trans. Daniel Haberman (Jerusalem: Feldheim, 2008), 783.

3 See Hirsch, comment to Leviticus 23:15.

4 Hirsch, comment to Deuteronomy 16:9, in *The Hirsch Chumash: Sefer Devarim*, trans. Daniel Haberman (Jerusalem: Feldheim, 2009), 358.

counting reminds us to view our wealth with gratitude to the One who made it possible and inspires us to see it as a blessing that God has entrusted to us so that we can serve God's purposes in the world.

The Power of the Moment

In contrast to other instances of halachically mandated day-counting, we may not simply keep track of the Omer period in our heads;[5] rather, we are commanded to count the days and weeks of the Omer in a formal ritual manner, orally and while standing, in part because doing so draws our attention to the spiritual significance of time.[6] We begin counting each night by reciting the following blessing:

בָּרוּךְ אַתָּה, יְיָ אֱלֹהֵינוּ, מֶלֶךְ הָעוֹלָם, אֲשֶׁר קִדְּשָׁנוּ
בְּמִצְוֹתָיו וְצִוָּנוּ עַל סְפִירַת הָעֹמֶר.

Baruch atah, Adonai Eloheinu, Melech haolam, asher kid'shanu b'mitzvotav v'tzivanu al s'firat haomer.

Our praise to You, Adonai our God, Sovereign of all, who hallows us with mitzvot, commanding us to count the Omer.[7]

---

5 Nachmanides (comment to Leviticus 23:15) notes that in cases where a person has an emission, he/she must count seven days to himself (*lo*)/herself (*lah*) before becoming pure (see Leviticus 15:13 and 15:28)—i.e., the person is required simply to keep track of the days, but not to count them aloud. The command to count the Omer, by contrast, is stated as *us'fartem lachem* ("for yourselves" in the plural), which, according to Nachmanides, indicates that the obligation is for each individual person to count the Omer orally.

6 See Rabbi Michael Rosensweig, quoted in David Shapiro, *Rabbi Joseph B. Soloveitchik on Pesach,* Sefirat ha-Omer *and* Shavu'ot (Brookline, MA: Rabbi Joseph B. Soloveitchik Institute, 2005), 149.

7 The liturgy for *S'firat HaOmer* is found in *Mishkan T'filah*, ed. Elyse D. Frishman (New York: CCAR Press, 2007), 570. This translation comes from *Mishkan T'filah;* throughout the rest of this volume an original, alternate translation is used for the same Hebrew.

During the first six days of counting, one should say:

Today is the (first / second / . . . sixth) day of the Omer.

From the seventh day onward, one should take care to mention both the days and the weeks,[8] in the following manner:

Today is the fifteenth day—two weeks and one day of the Omer.

Rabbi Joseph Soloveitchik teaches that this practice of verbally counting days and weeks makes us aware both of where we have been and where we are going, thus evoking a sense of movement from one state of being to another.[9] Time, in the Jewish consciousness, is purposeful and directed, ripe with potential, and filled with meaning. Yet even as we look toward the future, counting each day forces us to acknowledge and appreciate the significance of the moment. Every day presents us with the choice to stay where we are, to revert to where we have been, or to progress toward fulfilling our destiny. The classical law codes instruct us to count the Omer at night (when a Hebrew calendar day begins) so that each day is counted *in full*. This halachic requirement evokes an essential lesson of *S'firat HaOmer*: that every moment of our lives is consequential, that every moment counts.

---

8 This halachah is based on Abayei's statement: "It is a commandment to count the days, and it is a commandment to count the weeks" (Babylonian Talmud, *M'nachot* 66a). Maimonides (*Sefer HaMitzvot*, positive commandment 161) explains that the obligation to count both days and weeks composes one single commandment rather than two distinct commandments.

9 Shapiro, *Rabbi Joseph B. Soloveitchik on Pesach, Sefirat ha-Omer and Shavu'ot*, 151–52.

Spiritual Purification and Preparation

Counting the days from the Exodus to Sinai establishes a philosophical link between the two events, reminding us that freedom comes with responsibility: God redeemed us from Egyptian slavery not merely so we could be free, but rather so we would serve God and live by God's Torah. Because fulfilling the Torah is the purpose of a Jew's life, we should glorify the day on which Torah was given by counting the days in eager anticipation "as is done by one who waits for the coming of the human being he loves best and counts the days and hours."[10]

Just as a bride is given time to prepare for her wedding day by adorning herself in jewels,[11] so too the Jewish people were given the Omer period to ready themselves to receive the Torah. The *Zohar*, the central text of Kabbalah, teaches that while they were slaves in Egypt, the Israelites were under the evil influence of the "other side" (*sitra achra*), which rendered them spiritually impure. Although God liberated them from these dark forces on Passover, they still required time to purify themselves before becoming fit to receive the Torah. Pointing to a halachic principle that a ritually impure person must complete a period of seven days before becoming pure again,[12] Kabbalah scholar Isaiah Tishby explains that "the seven weeks of Counting the Omer are seen as the seven 'clean' intervals necessary before Israel can be purified from the remains of the uncleanness in Egypt."[13]

Modern life continues to be, as the Rabbis understood it, a perpetual struggle between *yetzer hara* (the evil inclination) and *yetzer*

---

10 Moses Maimonides, *Guide of the Perplexed* 3:43, trans. Shlomo Pines (Chicago: University of Chicago Press, 1963), 2:571.

11 See mishnah at Babylonian Talmud, *K'tubot* 57a and Rashi ad loc.

12 See note 5 above.

13 Isaiah Tishby, *The Wisdom of the Zohar: An Anthology of Texts* (Portland, OR: Littman Library of Jewish Civilization, 1989), 3:1241–42.

hatov (the good inclination). Occasionally the dark forces of the other side tempt us astray; like our ancestors, we too need to be purified. Fortunately, Judaism offers a way back into the light. The Chasidic master S'fat Emet teaches that "the doorway to redemption is opened in Nisan [at Passover]," but in order to walk through it, we first must do the difficult work of cleansing ourselves of spiritual impurity. The Omer is a "clarifying period" during which we have the opportunity to focus intently on strengthening our good character attributes, tempering our negative ones, improving our actions, and realigning our priorities.[14] In so doing, we prepare ourselves intellectually, emotionally, and spiritually to stand again at Sinai and renew our covenant with God each year at Shavuot.

In the kabbalistic tradition, this purification is achieved through daily contemplation of the seven lower *s'firot*, which, as Lawrence Kushner and Nehemiah Polen explain, constitute seven "dimensions of the divine psyche":

1. *Chesed*, "love," means unlimited expansion and inclusiveness.
2. *G'vurah*, "rigor," means the setting of boundaries.
3. *Tiferet*, "beauty," means balance or harmony.
4. *Netzach*, "victory," means commitment, eternity, and showing up.
5. *Hod*, "splendor," means the reverberation that comes from making definitions, as these definitions ripple outward throughout our perception of the world.
6. *Y'sod*, "foundation," means the joy of creation, the (almost) orgiastic pleasure that is the foundational moment in every project.

---

14 S'fat Emet, in *Likkut mi-Sifrei ha-Gaon ha-Kodesh Ba'al ha-"S'fat Emet" al Seder ha-T'filah* (Hebrew) (Jerusalem, 5767), 2:190.

7. *Malchut*, "kingdom," means receptivity to take in the blessing that is given.[15]

According to kabbalistic theory, all seven *s'firot* continuously act and react upon each other, creating dynamic spiritual energy within God. Because we are made in God's image, the same spiritual dynamism exists within us as well. To help us tap into it, kabbalistic practice sets each of the seven *s'firot* as the theme of one of the Omer's seven weeks: the first week's theme is *Chesed*, the second week's theme is *G'vurah*, and so on. On each day of the *Chesed* week, for example, we contemplate *Chesed* together with one of these seven *s'firot*, progressing from one *s'firah* to the next in the order enumerated above:

- On the first day, we ponder *Chesed* (love) in combination with *Chesed*—for example: What does it mean to be consumed and driven by boundless love? When have I felt this way? What are the practical implications for my life when I approach the world with unlimited expansion and inclusiveness?
- On the second day, we consider *Chesed* in combination with *G'vurah* (rigor): Why would I need to set boundaries on love? How do I know where those boundaries are, and how do I set them in practice? What happens if my boundaries are too loose or too firm?
- On the third day, we contemplate *Chesed* in combination with *Tiferet* (beauty): What makes love beautiful? How can love bring

---

15 Adapted from Lawrence Kushner and Nehemiah Polen, "Chasidic and Mystical Perspectives," in *My People's Prayer Book: Traditional Prayers, Modern Commentaries*, vol. 9, *Welcoming the Night*, ed. Lawrence A. Hoffman (Woodstock, VT: Jewish Lights, 2005), 169.

balance and harmony into my life and into the lives of others? Is it possible for love to create imbalance?

This method of reflection continues throughout the remainder of the forty-nine-day Omer period. Rabbi Laibl Wolf, a contemporary Chasidic writer and lecturer, teaches that these forty-nine combinations within the divine psyche correspond to forty-nine shades of emotions in the human personality.[16] To count the Omer using the kabbalistic method, therefore, is to engage in intense exploration of our own mind, character, and spirit in order to strengthen and elevate them.

Purifying ourselves spiritually during the Omer period raises us to a new level of holiness and enables us to commune with God on Shavuot.[17] As discussed above, the ancient omer offering that was brought at the beginning of the counting period was a sacrifice of barley; the Shavuot sacrifice marking the end of the Omer, by contrast, was a gift of wheat. These agricultural practices have profound spiritual meaning, as Hirsch explains:

> The omer is brought from *barley flour*. Barley, however, is not a primary food of man, but food for animals (see b. Sotah 14a). The omer, then, represents merely physical existence. . . . Only on the fiftieth day, after struggling to purification and freedom while counting the days and weeks; only on the day that commemorates

---

16 I heard Rabbi Wolf discuss these ideas at a Jewish Learning Institute Lecture in Skokie, Illinois, on August 26, 2012.

17 See S'fat Emet, s.v. *us'fartem lachem* (*Emor*, 652), 188, where he interprets the two loaves of bread that are commanded to be brought as a Shavuot offering (Leviticus 23:17) as an allusion to the fusion of divine and human spiritual forces on that festival.

the giving of the Torah, does Israel approach God's altar with *wheat* bread—which is designed for man.[18]

In short, Counting the Omer inspires us to do the hard work of spiritual purification—work that elevates us above an earthly, animal-like existence and helps us become more fully human.

Evolving Attitudes, Evolving Practices

Classical Concerns:
The Temple, Mourning Rituals, and Lag BaOmer

Although the omer sacrifice can no longer be offered in the absence of the Temple, the commandment of *S'firat HaOmer* remains obligatory as a *zeicher laMikdash*, an act performed in remembrance of the Temple's destruction.[19] As such, the Omer period, which was originally tied to the bounty of the harvest, has in the post-Temple era taken on a sad and somber character that, due to historical events, has deep-

---

18 Hirsch, comment to Leviticus 23:17. *The Hirsch Chumash: Sefer Vayikra*, 794.

19 Rabbi Joseph Soloveitchik teaches that there are two types of *zeicher laMikdash* (a ritual performed in remembrance of the Temple): One type of *zeicher laMikdash* recalls the glory and splendor of the Temple while it stood. This type, which includes the commandments to take the *lulav* on Sukkot and to blow the shofar on Rosh HaShanah, is a joyous kind of remembrance; for that reason, we say the *Shehecheyanu* blessing before performing these commandments. The second type of *zeicher laMikdash* recalls the Temple's destruction and, in contrast to the first type, has a mournful connotation. Soloveitchik contends that because the Sages did not ordain that we should say *Shehecheyanu* before counting the Omer, we can conclude that they understood the mitzvah of *S'firat HaOmer* in our time to be a *zeicher laMikdash* of the second, mournful type. For an extended discussion of this issue, see Shapiro, *Rabbi Joseph B. Soloveitchik on Pesach, Sefirat ha-Omer and Shavu'ot*, 135–37.

ened over time. According to the Talmud, thousands of Rabbi Akiva's disciples died during the days of the Omer of a plague brought on because they acted disrespectfully toward one another.[20] Other Jewish national tragedies have similarly occurred during the counting period, including massacres of German Jews by the Crusaders and the Nazi deportation of Hungarian Jews.[21] The halachah gives expression to this somber mood by requiring abstention from haircuts, weddings, and other joyous events from the beginning of the Omer until the thirty-third day (known as Lag BaOmer), since according to tradition, the suffering of Rabbi Akiva's disciples halted on that day.[22] Thus it is common for observant Jews to celebrate Lag BaOmer by having weddings, holding festive bonfires, and cutting their hair. Rabbi Isaac Klein adds that in modern times, Yom HaAtzma-ut (Israel's Independence Day), which occurs on the twentieth day of the Omer (5 Iyar), provides another festive interruption during the counting period. These days present opportunities for modern Reform Jews to celebrate and reflect on the themes of freedom, independence, and responsibility.

---

20 See Babylonian Talmud, *Y'vamot* 62b.

21 See Isaac Klein, *A Guide to Jewish Religious Practice* (New York: Ktav, 1992), 142–43.

22 See *Shulchan Aruch, Orach Chayim* 493:1–3. Rabbi Moses Isserles notes that weddings are permitted from Lag BaOmer through the end of the Omer period (493:1). Rabbi Joseph Caro holds that haircutting is prohibited through the end of Lag BaOmer, until the morning of the thirty-fourth day (493:2), but Isserles explains that in Ashkenazic lands, it is permitted to cut one's hair on Lag BaOmer itself (ad loc.). Isserles adds, however, that customs regarding haircutting vary from place to place: in some locales, people are accustomed to cutting their hair on the first of Iyar, whereas in other places, haircutting is prohibited until Lag BaOmer, but permitted thereafter (gloss to 493:3). Isaac Klein likewise notes variation in the mourning customs practiced during this period and explains that "in Ashkenazic communities, the most widespread custom has been to observe mourning from Pesah [*sic*] until three days before Shavuot. Exceptions are made on Rosh Hodesh Sivan, Rosh Hodesh Iyar, and Lag Ba'Omer" (Klein, *A Guide to Jewish Religious Practice*, 143).

Reform Attitudes and Practice: Then and Now

Reform Judaism, in the main, has abandoned the mourning practices associated with the Omer. An 1871 synod of early European Reform leaders formally abrogated the halachic ban on weddings during the Omer, and a 1913 American Reform responsum asserted that the prohibition was no longer religiously significant in light of scholarship demonstrating it to "have [its] parallel in ancient Roman superstition, or rather mythology."[23] Beyond this, Reform literature is largely silent as to why Counting the Omer fell out of practice. Liturgy for *S'firat HaOmer* is omitted without explanation from CCAR Reform prayer books prior to *Mishkan T'filah*, and *Gates of the Seasons: A Guide to the Jewish Year* likewise contains no mention of the practice. One possible reason is that in its original biblical context, there is no indication that Counting the Omer had any purpose other than to ensure that the Shavuot festival, marking the harvest's end, would be celebrated on the proper day. For this reason, explained Rabbi Mark Washofsky in 2001, "Reform Judaism has [in the past] generally regarded this 'counting' as a regulation of the calendar"—that is, a utilitarian activity without spiritual significance—and thus concluded that "there is no need . . . to count the days in a ritual manner."[24]

But we are in a new era of our Movement, in which it is common for Reform congregations and individuals to reclaim traditional practices once discarded by previous generations for whom they lacked resonance.

---

23 K. Kohler and D. Neumark, "Times When Weddings Should Not Take Place," in *American Reform Responsa*, ed. Walter Jacob (New York: CCAR Press, 1983), 410.

24 Mark Washofsky, *Jewish Living: A Guide to Contemporary Reform Practice* (New York: URJ Press, 2001), 110. In the 2010 edition of his book (p. 109), Washofsky notes the inclusion of *S'firat HaOmer* in the new CCAR prayer book *Mishkan T'filah*, indicating that this previous Reform attitude has begun to change.

Reform Judaism is defined by its commitment to change, and as some of our Movement's leading voices have put it, "Nothing would, therefore, hinder us as Reform Jews from readopting customs once omitted if a new generation finds them meaningful and useful in its practice of Judaism."[25] Movement in this direction is already evident: the newest CCAR prayer book, *Mishkan T'filah*, published in 2007, includes liturgy for Counting the Omer, as does *Mishkan Moeid: A Guide to the Jewish Seasons* (2013), which is meant to replace *Gates of the Seasons*.[26] In this proud tradition of change, Rabbi Kedar aims to help us rediscover and reinvent *S'firat HaOmer* in a way that embodies the contemporary Reform spirit. Taking inspiration from Chasidic tradition, which sees these days between Passover and Shavuot as "good days [*yamim tovim*], like *chol hamo-eid* [the intermediate days of a festival], because there is holiness before them and after them,"[27] she gives us access to *S'firat HaOmer* as a modern spiritual practice, focused not on sadness and mourning, but rather on contemplation and reflection, inner exploration, and spiritual growth.

The Aim of This Book

Rabbi Marc-Alain Ouaknin, quoting Emanuel Levinas, has written:

> A Book is worthy of this name . . . if its "power of saying goes beyond its intention of saying," if it "contains more than it contains." . . . The book is a Book if it is the source of the opening of a mouth, if it creates and generates speech.[28]

25 Walter Jacob et al., "Discarded Practices," in *American Reform Responsa*, 4.

26 See note 7 above.

27 S'fat Emet, s.v., *us'fartem lachem* (*Emor*, 642), 187.

28 Marc-Alain Ouaknin, *The Burnt Book: Reading the Talmud*, trans. Llewellyn Brown (Princeton, NJ: Princeton University Press, 1995), 156, 170.

This book is a modern liturgy for Counting the Omer. The poetry and prose contained in these pages are meant to inspire, but what they will say to you—and how you will respond—is not yet known. They are presented here without commentary. The hope is that as you contemplate and meditate on the words, they will reveal messages your soul needs to hear and help guide you on the path toward your unique destiny. May your counting this year be transformational, may this book be worthy of its name, and "may the words of my mouth and the meditations of my heart be acceptable to You, Adonai, my Rock and my Redeemer" (Psalm 19:15).

Before We Begin

Three Levels of Holiday Observance

I once learned that each Jewish holiday and festival has three levels of meaning, and if we ignore any one of these dimensions, then we have not fully participated, celebrated, and considered its significance.

The first dimension is historical. We must understand and acknowledge the events and circumstances that created the moment of celebration or commemoration. Because Counting the Omer begins on Passover (the holiday of freedom) and ends on Shavuot (the holiday of receiving the Torah from Sinai), there is an association with the historical theme of the journey from slavery to liberation, from wandering in the desert to revelation at Mount Sinai.

The second dimension is based on the Land of Israel. While history connects us to specific points in time, Israel connects us to a sense of place. Jewish holidays relate to agricultural, cultural, or historical events. In biblical times, Counting the Omer was a commandment to count each day of a seven-week period between the barley harvest and the wheat harvest. During this period, the Israelites would make pilgrimages to Jerusalem bringing sheaves (the word *omer* can be translated as "sheaf," denoting a quantity, a dry measure used for grains) to the Temple as an offering of thanksgiving for the abundance and bounty: "You shall count from the eve of the second day of Pesach, when an omer of grain is to be brought as an offering, seven complete weeks. The day after the seventh week of your counting will make fifty days, and you shall present a new meal offering to Adonai" (Leviticus 23:15–16).

1

The spiritual overlay of the historical and agricultural adds a third dimension to celebration and commemoration. Rabbi A. Brian Stoller, in his introduction to this book, mentions the interpretation that the kabbalists gave to the obligation to count the Omer. No longer living in the Land and reaping its bounty, they emphasized the spiritual possibilities of the practice. They lifted Counting the Omer above the earthly commandment of land, harvest, and pilgrimage and elevated it to mystical contemplation and practice.

History and land bind us to time and place, whereas the spiritual dimension bids us to experience, transcend, and aspire. This book focuses on the spiritual level. The daily counting has power when used as a practice for contemplation. In his book *The Eternal Journey: Meditations on the Jewish Year*, Rabbi Jonathan Wittenberg writes:

> The laws regarding the Omer are very strict: every day matters and not one may be missed. Not to waste a single day should be our ideal in life. . . . In general we could perhaps say that a day is wasted when we've done nothing that brings happiness or good to others and nothing that brings a sense of purpose to ourselves.

Sustained daily, contemplation and consideration enable us to focus our attention and heighten our awareness toward the importance and sacred energy of our lives. We count, and in doing so make an accounting of who we are and what we want. The daily rhythm makes this a practice, and the intentional internal accounting makes it a spiritual practice. Perhaps spiritual practice is an apt translation for today's expression of *avodah,* often translated as "prayer." It is indeed hard work to take upon ourselves a consistent, intentional, and disciplined practice. Forty-nine days, seven weeks of sustained attention to living with purpose can have a great healing and uplifting effect.

In addition, this particular period of time between Passover and Shavuot is rich with metaphor and symbolism and provides a powerful framework for spiritual exploration. The counting begins with the escape from enslavement to the wandering path of freedom, which leads to a mystical encounter with God, Sinai, and Torah. It is therefore a fitting structure for a personal journey toward meaningful and purposeful living.

Seven Weeks, Seven Principles

For forty-nine days, or seven weeks, we take on a discipline, an obligation to mindfully enter the day, to be aware of its potential power to matter, to make a difference, to count for something. Awaken your routine with intention, with attention.

Our tradition often engages in what I call a spiritual mapping of the universe. These are lists, a series of spiritual principles that sustain and guide the spiritual world. It seems we have engaged in mapping from the times of the Bible throughout Rabbinic literature. We learn from the prophets (Micah 5), from the Mishnah (*Avot* 3:1, 4:17, 5:1), from the Talmud (*Shabbat* 31a), from Musar literature (*midot*)—to name just a few. Our tradition is not dogmatic; never do the Rabbis believe that the list they teach is the only way to spiritual enlightenment, but rather that there are spiritual laws that govern our lives and many ways to achieve enlightenment.

And so I offer an original set of seven spiritual principles for the seven weeks of the Omer: decide, discern, choose, hope, imagine, courage, pray. Each day has a text mined from contemporary and classical literature, with a thought from me. Making sense of the connections between texts and themes is not always obvious, and the work of discovery is an important part of your own personal journey. These principles are points of light to illuminate a path toward spiritual awareness. Each one, powerful on its own, can be a sort of North Star, as you count each day, each week.

Week One: *decide.* With fortitude, determination, and focus we can decide that the way we are living, thinking, behaving no longer serves us, and it is time to try another way. This is not a small matter. We try to shift from familiar and comfortable patterns. We find ourselves affirming our decisions and refining them over and over. As quickly as we decide to embark on a path, we often become confused. It is a continual cycle. So many voices prevail upon our good intentions. Which voice to listen to? And to what end?

Week Two: *discern.* Sort through the advice of friends and the echoes of your parents. Understand what helps and what doesn't and sort, choosing what to keep, what to discard. Question your well-guarded assumptions, and challenge the pervasive fear of doing the wrong thing. Discernment is clarity. It is fine-tuning. It is guidance. It is trusting intuition over fear, listening to the gentle fluttering of longing and to the whispers of the soul. It is self-reliance. It is the utter denial of negativity and the commitment to positive thinking. And yet, discernment is not dogmatic; there are a myriad of possibilities to self-actualize, to discover purpose, to have a meaningful life, to impact our world, making it safer and more compassionate.

Week Three: *choose.* To choose! To acknowledge! To affirm! Choice is empowerment when we choose to live differently, to be better. With every choice we defy inertia, with every choice we expand our sense of possibility. With every choice we become emboldened. But it isn't easy, nor is it linear. We go back and forth between choice and discernment, reaffirming our decisions, reexamining everything. The spiritual path is a zigzag, a switchback up a mountain. It is exhausting, riddled with doubt and setbacks. There are so many ways to get us to where we need to go.

Week Four: *hope.* Anticipating, believing, affirming, thinking abundantly, even when our self-confidence is not strong. Hope takes practice. When the human spirit aspires, we stretch. When we reach beyond what enslaves us, we live with light and goodness. When hope becomes the answer to fear, so much is possible. Imagine the possibilities when we envision ourselves as strong, healthy, loving. Miracles abound.

Week Five: *imagine.* To have an expansive and abundant way of seeing the world. To see the invisible. To live with possibility and vision. To see ourselves as a miracle, a daily revelation of goodness. We are limited only by our imagination. And what *if* that were true? Where would your imagination lead you? What magnificence might you manifest?

Week Six: *courage.* Courage to live. Courage to love. Courage to risk. Courage to fail. And patience. It takes time to become the person we want to be, to grow and unfold, to fail and persevere. There is a vastness between what is possible and what is real; an expanse of uncertainty, ambiguity, and doubt. When we are afraid, we are paralyzed, suspended in midair between imagination and manifestation. It is the natural course of things to have our dreams lay fallow; only care and determination make the ground rich and ready to bear fruit. When we see our limitations as failure, we are afraid. Be brave and step into your life.

Week Seven: *pray.* Sometimes our power lies within our ability to let go of our delusions of control. By offering a prayer, we confess the boundaries of our power to know and to understand everything. Through prayer we find the strength to decide, to change. Within our prayers we sense the inner stirring of discernment, and we find the guidance to choose well. Within our prayers we find the light of hope and the imagination to dream. Within our prayers we find the courage to sustain our path when doubt casts a shadow. Through prayer we find faith. When we pray, we partner with some invisible force that leads us toward our destiny, to the freedoms we so desire. Prayer is a conversation with the invisible. It expands the reality in which we live and bids us to imagine holiness, eternity, love, goodness, and beauty.

Special Days

For forty-nine days we elevate each day with intention, contemplation, and attention. And then there are days that have an added significance such as holidays, memorial days, and Shabbat. Some of these days are linked to the Jewish calendar and some to the secular calendar. I have included an additional section of these special days that occur during the Omer, so that alongside the daily counting, when a day of special significance occurs, you can linger a bit longer with an additional reading.

The Personal Journey: An Invitation

Come let us consider together.
(Isaiah 1:18)

Dawn. Color peeks above the horizon, washing the edge of the world with splendor, glorious hues that beckon us to live brightly, bravely, unabashed.

Sometimes the sun rises suddenly in a blaze of white. It startles the unsuspecting soul, and it is overpowering, blinding. We turn away, though out of the corner of our eye and upon the softness of our face we secretly feel its warmth.

And then sometimes the sun humbly rises, without spectacle, without color, without the drama of dawn. Simply light. The darkness dissipates. Our tender views are revealed. And we are called upon to live our life's purpose and to believe in the beauty we now see.

And so often the sun rises when we sleep. Its miracle not seen, not noticed, not blessed. We awake, and it is day. We go about our morning. Routine.

This is how we live our days. At times grateful for the beauty, at times wary of the intensity, sometimes gently, and then at times completely unaware of the gifts offered each precious day. Come with me . . . let us count the days ahead, each one considered, each one light upon the dawn, humble, tenderly revealing an inner light, strength, the courage to live. These days are filled with power. They offer an archetype, the path from enslavement to freedom, darkness to light, constriction to expanse.

So much life and love swirl within our dreams. How we yearn to be brave, to find our way around obstacles, to have faith, to run toward the future fortified with hope, to not fear the wilderness of uncertainty!

So much possibility.

As we grow, we deepen. And as we deepen, we stretch. And as we stretch, our capacity for love expands, healing us. And as we heal, we are compelled to heal the world.

Slavery. The story of the Exodus from Egypt is universal and it is epic and it is an archetype that spans across the centuries. It is a deeply personal story. The Children of Israel stand at the edge of the wilderness and beckon us to become a part of a mixed multitude marching toward freedom. Their march, their courage and their doubt, touch our well-protected self, which tugs and pokes around our soul.

So much enslaves us. We are enslaved by our assumptions of what is possible. We are enslaved by the words we use, the constructs of our thoughts and speech, the way we explain the past and speak about the future. We are enslaved by our presumed limitations. We are enslaved by negativity and cynicism. We are enslaved by our fear. Escape is lifelong, complicated, thrilling. It is the substance of growth and self-actualization.

We venture forth if we decide to. Though we are not alone, our journey is solitary.

And here is an undeniable truth. We will not change until we want to change. And even then . . .

Freedom. To decide, to affirm, to choose. Freedom can be maddening. And frightening. Where to go? How do we discern the correct path? So many possibilities, the wilderness is so vast . . . Slavery's master was known, predicable, authoritative; what invisible force is the master of freedom? Freedom cannot be willy-nilly; it cannot be wild abandonment, self-centered, untethered. To be free is to live the religious paradoxes of choice and destiny, of independence and obligation, of memory and vision, of self-fulfillment and communal responsibility. When tethered, freedom lifts us toward holiness, wonder, aspiration, and meaning.

> *Blessed is God who has drawn me out of Egypt and led me to his chambers in loving grace.*
>
> *As promised, I will go to the mountain of God, to the house of prayer and rejoice.*

Based on Song of Songs 1 (*P'sikta Zutarta, Lekach Tov*)

8

Week One:

Decide

Moses asked, *Who am I that I should go? . . .*
And God said, *I will be with you.*

Exodus 3:11–12

God calls Moses to his destiny, with an inextinguishable light. Doubt casts a shadow. We imagine him quivering, afraid, trying to avoid and protest the call. How familiar is this moment? Self-doubt plagues even the most accomplished and seemingly confident person. It prevents us from walking upon the path to self-actualization. *Am I worthy? Am I able? Am I good enough?*

So often, the problem is not the call but rather the response. The twin enemies fatigue and fear are ever pervasive, making us unconscious to possibility, to beauty, to our capacity for excellence and splendor. Daily we wander through life undirected, unnoticed, and unannounced by the grandeur of our spirit. We may be fine, but that tolerance for mediocrity places us in a fog. Voices convince us that our limitations matter more than anything. We are tired. We are so afraid of so many things. We simply do not see the power of decision.

But when we are fearless, we fly; when we reach beyond our limitations, we grow; when we say yes to living, we live. And upon saying yes, possibility abounds—the possibility of reclaimed power, of self-realization, of abundant living, of becoming who we were meant to be.

16 NISAN

1st Day of the Omer

Early one morning I raised my sails and tacked out of the canal, not sure where I wanted to go. When I reached the open water, I decided not to cross the bay to the barrier beach, as was my custom, but to hug the mainland. I turned eastward toward the climbing sun and made a long run past familiar landmarks. . . .

The heat of August was on the land and a rich, deep foliage covered the shore. Through the leaves I could see occasional signs of civilization: a chimney, a gas tank, a water tower, a church steeple. I lived there, along with thousands of others, somewhere beyond the tree line in that suburban town. But from the sea, under the sail of my sloop, the coast looked sparsely settled, barely touched by human habitation and still pristine. . . .

But as soon as I reached the open water, I found myself faced with a familiar dilemma; this freedom I cherished came with a precondition: I had to decide where I wanted to go.

Richard Bode, *First You Have to Row a Little Boat:*
Reflections on Life & Living

Life is like a symphony: a complexity of harmony, rhythm, and resonance all combine to create the sounds and pauses, the rise and fall of a life well lived. And daily, we step onto the stage and play, and the sound we make in this world is ours, created from practice, skill, and heart. And some days are better than others. Sometimes we are not at our best, the sound is off, the energy is low, the crowd is unresponsive, our heart is just not into it. And sometimes we are better than good, feeling focused, magnificent, connecting to all things and everyone. Alas, sometimes they throw flowers, and sometimes they throw tomatoes.

Never mind. I was once taught: you are never as good as they say you are, and you are never as bad as they say you are.

All that matters is that each day, we create anew the possibility of a joyful sound unto God.

בָּרוּךְ אַתָּה, יְיָ אֱלֹהֵינוּ, מֶלֶךְ הָעוֹלָם, אֲשֶׁר קִדְּשָׁנוּ
בְּמִצְוֹתָיו וְצִוָּנוּ עַל סְפִירַת הָעֹמֶר.

Baruch atah, Adonai Eloheinu, Melech haolam, asher kid'shanu
b'mitzvotav v'tzivanu al s'firat haomer.

Praised be You, Adonai our God, who rules the universe,
instilling within us the holiness of mitzvot by commanding us
to count the Omer.

Today is the first day of the Omer.

2nd Day of the Omer

Change is difficult, not simply because it is a journey into the unknown but because we grow restless and unsure of ourselves too easily. We moan like children: "Why aren't we there yet?" . . .

. . . You may be thinking "After I feel better, then I'll use my gifts," or "I'll look for my gifts the next time I'm in trouble." You can choose to think of your gifts only as emergency first aid, but if you do, you're missing the point. If you recognize them as the constant companions they are, they can not only restore your peace after it has been broken; they can provide support so that your life never falls apart again.

Robin L. Silverman, *The Ten Gifts*

We change when we decide to change, and we grow when we decide to grow. Decision is the consciousness that we must try another way. When we decide to be better, we are. When we decide to embark on a path of greatness, we do. When we decide to live another way, we can. When we realize that every day we are once again invited to live a life of beauty, then we need only say yes.

בָּרוּךְ אַתָּה, יְיָ אֱלֹהֵינוּ, מֶלֶךְ הָעוֹלָם, אֲשֶׁר קִדְּשָׁנוּ
בְּמִצְוֹתָיו וְצִוָּנוּ עַל סְפִירַת הָעֹמֶר.

Baruch atah, Adonai Eloheinu, Melech haolam, asher kid'shanu b'mitzvotav v'tzivanu al s'firat haomer.

Praised be You, Adonai our God, who rules the universe, instilling within us the holiness of mitzvot by commanding us to count the Omer.

Today is the second day of the Omer.

18   NISAN

3rd Day of the Omer

It's funny: I always imagined when I was a kid that adults had some kind of inner toolbox, full of shiny tools: the saw of discernment, the hammer of wisdom, the sandpaper of patience. But then when I grew up I found that life handed you these rusty bent old tools—friendships, prayer, conscience, honesty—and said, Do the best you can with these, they will have to do. And mostly, against all odds, they're enough.

Anne Lamott, *Traveling Mercies: Some Thoughts on Faith*

My father once told me that a person is judged by three things. "First is a good name," he said. "Integrity and a good name are really all we have in life." He continued, "You must also have a sense of humor." Then he looked at me with kindness and love and said, "And dear, you need to work on yours."

Years passed.

And one day I found myself telling someone his words of wisdom, but when I came to the third thing by which we are judged, I realized I had forgotten what it was. So I asked my father, and he too had forgotten. So I set off on a journey in search of the third principle by which my life will be judged.

It's been quite a journey so far. Have compassion as I try to figure it out, and in the meantime, judge gently of me.

בָּרוּךְ אַתָּה, יְיָ אֱלֹהֵינוּ, מֶלֶךְ הָעוֹלָם, אֲשֶׁר קִדְּשָׁנוּ
בְּמִצְוֹתָיו וְצִוָּנוּ עַל סְפִירַת הָעֹמֶר.

Baruch atah, Adonai Eloheinu, Melech haolam, asher kid'shanu
b'mitzvotav v'tzivanu al s'firat haomer.

Praised be You, Adonai our God, who rules the universe,
instilling within us the holiness of mitzvot by commanding us
to count the Omer.

Today is the third day of the Omer.

My soul is quiet,
Awaiting God.

PSALM 62:2

4th Day of the Omer

Most people assume that our breathing function is a two-part rhythm of exhalation and inhalation, but this is not the case. The breathing rhythm has three components: the exhalation, a pause, and the inhalation. The pause gives us a rest from the effort of the exhalation, and enables us to rally the energy needed for the next inhalation. The pause is not an idle period when nothing happens, but a vital phase in the breathing process.

If we interfere with the length of the breathing pause, shortening it even slightly, we find ourselves feeling rushed and pressured. A full-length pause in your breathing rhythm will have a calming effect and engender a feeling of relief, eradicating the sensation of being under pressure. However you should not try to make the pause willfully, as its duration must vary with your different breathing needs at different times. What you should do is to try to become aware of any ways in which you might be inhibiting the pause, thereby generating feelings of stress.

Avraham Greenbaum, *Under the Table & How to Get Up:*
Jewish Pathways of Spiritual Growth

Today I promise to breathe.

With the change of a vowel, the Hebrew word for breath, *n'shimah*, is the same as the word for soul, *n'shamah*. Breath connects body and soul. Think of the words we use—our lives are spiritful when we aspire, inspire, and conspire. Until soul and body part and we expire.

This is the meaning of spirituality. The enlivenment of your spirit. Aspire, and fill your mind and heart with loveliness. Inspiration abounds. Open your eyes to beauty and breath in an unending spirit, eternally present. Conspire, with others, connecting with those who agree to create a life, elegant with spiritual intention.

So, for all this and more, and with gratitude for life, today commit to conscious breath.

בָּרוּךְ אַתָּה, יְיָ אֱלֹהֵינוּ, מֶלֶךְ הָעוֹלָם, אֲשֶׁר קִדְּשָׁנוּ
בְּמִצְוֹתָיו וְצִוָּנוּ עַל סְפִירַת הָעֹמֶר.

Baruch atah, Adonai Eloheinu, Melech haolam, asher kid'shanu
b'mitzvotav v'tzivanu al s'firat haomer.

Praised be You, Adonai our God, who rules the universe,
instilling within us the holiness of mitzvot by commanding us
to count the Omer.

Today is the fourth day of the Omer.

20 NISAN

5th Day of the Omer

A voice calls out: "You must!"
Must what? O voice, explain!
Instead of an answer I hear
That call again.

I peer behind the door,
I dash at every wall;
I search, though no one strange
Has sent that call.

I've known them all my life,
The caller and his call,
Yet it seems to me I hear
What I never heard at all.

It cries: "You must! You must!"
And only God can tell
Whether *must* is my redemption,
Or *must* will be my hell.

"A Voice Calls Out" by H. Leivick,
translated by Cynthia Ozick, in *A Treasury of Yiddish Poetry*,
edited by Irving Howe and Eliezer Greenberg

Live your life as if it were a command, an imperative from some great and mighty force that demands that your time and attention not be squandered. This is what is called living fearlessly, for shallowness, apathy, and boredom take over our lives when we become meek and forgetful.

So remember, you were born for greatness, and the world is in desperate need of your loving attention.

בָּרוּךְ אַתָּה, יְיָ אֱלֹהֵינוּ, מֶלֶךְ הָעוֹלָם, אֲשֶׁר קִדְּשָׁנוּ בְּמִצְוֹתָיו וְצִוָּנוּ עַל סְפִירַת הָעֹמֶר.

Baruch atah, Adonai Eloheinu, Melech haolam, asher kid'shanu b'mitzvotav v'tzivanu al s'firat haomer.

Praised be You, Adonai our God, who rules the universe, instilling within us the holiness of mitzvot by commanding us to count the Omer.

Today is the fifth day of the Omer.

Do not recall what happened before,
do not dwell on the past.
I am about to do something new;
It shall flourish, you will see!
I will forge a path through the desert,
and rivers shall flow in the wilderness.

Isaiah 43:18–19

21 NISAN

6th Day of the Omer

What I learned is the difference between destiny and fate. We are all fated to die. Destiny is recognizing the radiance of the soul that, even when faced with human impossibility, loves all of life. Fate is the death we owe to Nature. Destiny is the life we owe to soul.

Marion Woodman, *Bone: Dying into Life*

When we are young we are led to believe that our legacy lies in our successes and our failures. And so life becomes a game, a sort of tally of victories and failures. We keep score of triumphant moments and try to minimize, leverage, and rebrand the not-so-successful moments. All the while we hope and often pray that the endgame will be to our advantage and we will be proclaimed a great success. But that is only partially true.

Our most abiding legacy lies within the strength of our character. And it may just be an ironic twist of fate that character is best built and measured when we experience conflict, adversity, and failure. Not that success is without its test of courage and integrity. But when we fail— and we all do—we experience a profound moment of loss, which is layered and nuanced. In failure, we may lose the game we are playing, our work, our livelihood, a relationship, a power struggle. And even more crippling, we may lose confidence, a positive self-image, optimism, stability, good cheer, which knocks us off-balance, off our mark. Herein lies the test of character: in the effort to regain composure, balance, direction, our footing. How we react, respond, rebound is a measure of our inner strength, our character, our fortitude, our inner vision of what is possible despite the outer collapse of what was.

It is in the motion of regaining balance that the strength of our character is formed, forged, and molded.

בָּרוּךְ אַתָּה, יְיָ אֱלֹהֵינוּ, מֶלֶךְ הָעוֹלָם, אֲשֶׁר קִדְּשָׁנוּ בְּמִצְוֹתָיו וְצִוָּנוּ עַל סְפִירַת הָעֹמֶר.

Baruch atah, Adonai Eloheinu, Melech haolam, asher kid'shanu b'mitzvotav v'tzivanu al s'firat haomer.

Praised be You, Adonai our God, who rules the universe, instilling within us the holiness of mitzvot by commanding us to count the Omer.

Today is the sixth day of the Omer.

22 NISAN

7th Day of the Omer

The mockingbird took a single step into the air and dropped. His wings were still folded against his sides as though he were singing from a limb and not falling, accelerating thirty-two feet per second, through empty air. Just a breath before he would have been dashed to the ground, he unfurled his wings with exact, deliberate care, revealing the broad bars of white, spread his elegant, white-banded tail, and so floated onto the grass. I had just rounded a corner when his insouciant step caught my eye; there was no one else in sight. The fact of his free fall was like the old philosophical conundrum about the tree that falls in the forest. The answer must be, I think, that beauty and grace are performed whether or not we will or sense them. The least we can do is try to be there.

Annie Dillard, *Pilgrim at Tinker Creek*

I wonder, what if I remove the thin gray film that has covered my eyes? I wonder. And if I became determined, really resolved, what would I know, what would I see?

And I wonder, how is it that inertia is more powerful than transformation and why do I constantly settle when anything could be, and how is it that risk frightens me, because staying the same is so un-extraordinary.

And I wonder . . .

if I dare to be.

בָּרוּךְ אַתָּה, יְיָ אֱלֹהֵינוּ, מֶלֶךְ הָעוֹלָם, אֲשֶׁר קִדְּשָׁנוּ
בְּמִצְוֹתָיו וְצִוָּנוּ עַל סְפִירַת הָעֹמֶר.

Baruch atah, Adonai Eloheinu, Melech haolam, asher kid'shanu
b'mitzvotav v'tzivanu al s'firat haomer.

Praised be You, Adonai our God, who rules the universe,
instilling within us the holiness of mitzvot by commanding us
to count the Omer.

Today is the seventh day—one week of the Omer.

DECIDE

Today I decide
to turn my eyes toward wonder,
so that I may see the expanse before me.

Today I decide to see the possibility of my life,
so that I may open my mind to greatness.

Today I will do one kindness,
so that my heart may become more loving.

Today I will pause to consider,
so that my life may become more deliberate.

Help me, dear God, to step
firmly upon a path of consequence,
so that I may make my life a prayer
of goodness and mercy, splendor and light.

I ask for a life of meaning,
a sense of purpose.
Today I decide.

Week Two:

Discern

And Moses asked, *When they ask me, "What is God's name?" what shall I say?*
And God answered, *Tell them that Ehyeh-Asher-Ehyeh,* I am and I will be, *sent me to you.*

Exodus 3:13–14

And when Moses searched for the words, the name, to describe the voice of the spirit, he discerned the truth of all true revelation and that our understanding of it is ever evolving and becoming. Tell them *I am and I will be*, God answered.

The voices inside our being confound. They chatter away, telling us what to do, where to go. The decision to step onto the path creates a problem. Which way do we turn? And with every voice, there are so many possibilities, and for every possibility, there are so many consequences. It can be maddening. And so we give in to the stupor of unconscious living; not knowing where to turn, we silence the voices that would guide us.

Consider the sounds and sights that surround you, the people who enter your inner circle, the patterns that make your days. Not all that is said is useful, not all that is learned is helpful, and not all who call us "friend" love us.

Discernment is the practice of sorting out the words and assumptions, tendencies and habits, people and surroundings. It is a primary principle of our spiritual life.

Like the farmer separates wheat from stalk and grain from chaff, a discerning heart examines, scrutinizes, searches, sorts, and sifts. Living well is a process; it takes refinement and practice.

That which is life-draining must fall away. And all that is life affirming is the foundation of a life well lived.

23 NISAN

8th Day of the Omer

Whatever anyone else says or does, I must be true to myself, just as if gold or emerald or the color purple would say, "Whatever anyone may do or say, I must be an emerald and keep my color."

In the universe, respect the highest power, namely the creative force that directs and makes use of all things. In the same way you must respect the highest power in yourself, for it is of the same creative kind.

For this is what makes use of the rest of you, and directs your life.

The Spiritual Teachings of Marcus Aurelius,
translated by Mark Forstater

Once I was walking down the streets of Jerusalem. It was hot. A dusty desert storm covered the sky. To the undiscerning eye, it was cloudy. But I knew that above the sandy haze were the sun, the sky, the blue, the summer heat. No clouds. Just sand particles from a place far away and unknown. But I shrugged. Because down here, on the street, it was coarse and slightly dim, and in the moment, that was what mattered most.

What is it that we know for sure? The experience of dust and grit in our mouths, or the reality of blue, enduring, though beyond what we can see?

בָּרוּךְ אַתָּה, יְיָ אֱלֹהֵינוּ, מֶלֶךְ הָעוֹלָם, אֲשֶׁר קִדְּשָׁנוּ
בְּמִצְוֹתָיו וְצִוָּנוּ עַל סְפִירַת הָעֹמֶר.

Baruch atah, Adonai Eloheinu, Melech haolam, asher kid'shanu
b'mitzvotav v'tzivanu al s'firat haomer.

Praised be You, Adonai our God, who rules the universe,
instilling within us the holiness of mitzvot by commanding us
to count the Omer.

Today is the eighth day—one week and one day of the Omer.

We often say the right thing, and then find ourselves resenting having to do the right thing. Talk is cheap, however; our behavior is what truly defines us. Listen carefully to your speech; say only what you mean, and do everything you say.

This requires you to slow down your normal pace of communication. So often we talk just to talk. We say things for the sake of saying things. We exaggerate to make what we say more interesting. We promise things before we have determined whether or not we can fulfill the promise.

Ask yourself three questions before you speak:

1. Is it true?
2. Is it kind?
3. Is it necessary?

Rabbi Rami Shapiro, *The Sacred Art of Lovingkindness:*
Preparing to Practice

This is the obligation of a religious life:
We must give away our time, give away our money, and give away our
   kindness.
Life is purposeful when we give—
change a little corner of the world; make living a bit easier for a stranger;
   place a hand upon the shoulder of your neighbor.

בָּרוּךְ אַתָּה, יְיָ אֱלֹהֵינוּ, מֶלֶךְ הָעוֹלָם, אֲשֶׁר קִדְּשָׁנוּ
בְּמִצְוֹתָיו וְצִוָּנוּ עַל סְפִירַת הָעֹמֶר.

*Baruch atah, Adonai Eloheinu, Melech haolam, asher kid'shanu
b'mitzvotav v'tzivanu al s'firat haomer.*

Praised be You, Adonai our God, who rules the universe,
instilling within us the holiness of mitzvot by commanding us
to count the Omer.

Today is the ninth day—one week and two days of the Omer.

10th Day of the Omer

Sometimes the mountain
is hidden from me in veils
of cloud, sometimes
I am hidden from the mountain
in veils of inattention, apathy, fatigue,
when I forget or refuse to go
down to the shore or a few yards
up the road, on a clear day,
to reconfirm
that witnessing presence.

"Witness" by Denise Levertov, in *Evening Train*

Your life is a dance, defined by three small steps:
the times you step forward,
the times you step back,
and the times you hold your ground.

To know when to reach and when to yield takes years of practice, years
of prayer.
To know when to be still takes even longer.

בָּרוּךְ אַתָּה, יְיָ אֱלֹהֵינוּ, מֶלֶךְ הָעוֹלָם, אֲשֶׁר קִדְּשָׁנוּ
בְּמִצְוֹתָיו וְצִוָּנוּ עַל סְפִירַת הָעֹמֶר.

Baruch atah, Adonai Eloheinu, Melech haolam, asher kid'shanu
b'mitzvotav v'tzivanu al s'firat haomer.

Praised be You, Adonai our God, who rules the universe,
instilling within us the holiness of mitzvot by commanding us
to count the Omer.

Today is the tenth day—one week and three days of the Omer.

Send Your light and Your truth
And they shall lead me.

Psalm 43:3

26 NISAN

11th Day of the Omer

You *can* think too much, which is something Dante and his guide, Virgil, discovered on their outing to the Inferno. They were not permitted to pass through one particular threshold until they left all reason and intellect behind. These faculties are useful, in other words, but only up to a point. Beyond that, the door will be barred to us if we attempt to cross by way of reason. No amount of intellectual authority, arrogant confidence, name dropping, or ego and ambition pounding on the door demanding to be admitted will allow us passage. Beyond a certain point, faith is the magic lamp and humility the abracadabra.

Faith begins, if it begins at all, where knowledge leaves off.

Gregg Levoy, *Callings:*
Finding and Following an Authentic Life

Divine guidance is a whisper, a small and tender knowing that nestles in your being. Sometimes your mind hears it, sometimes your heart. Sometimes you are guided in words, sometimes in a sensation of well-being. But you know. You just know.

Listening takes practice; that is why we say *Sh'ma* twice daily. To pay attention is a command of consciousness.

Awaken!

בָּרוּךְ אַתָּה, יְיָ אֱלֹהֵינוּ, מֶלֶךְ הָעוֹלָם, אֲשֶׁר קִדְּשָׁנוּ
בְּמִצְוֹתָיו וְצִוָּנוּ עַל סְפִירַת הָעֹמֶר.

Baruch atah, Adonai Eloheinu, Melech haolam, asher ḳid'shanu
b'mitzvotav v'tzivanu al s'firat haomer.

Praised be You, Adonai our God, who rules the universe,
instilling within us the holiness of mitzvot by commanding us
to count the Omer.

Today is the eleventh day—one week and four days of the Omer.

27   NISAN

12th Day of the Omer

Martin Buber tells this tale: "Rabbi Mendel once boasted to his teacher Rabbi Elimelekh that evenings he saw the angel who rolls away the light before the darkness, and mornings the angel who rolls away the darkness before the light. 'Yes,' said Rabbi Elimelekh, 'in my youth I saw that too. Later on you don't see these things anymore.'" . . .

Seeing is of course very much a matter of verbalization. Unless I call my attention to what passes before my eyes, I simply won't see it. It is, as Ruskin says, "not merely unnoticed, but in the full, clear sense of the word, unseen." My eyes alone can't solve analogy tests using figures, the ones which show, with increasing elaborations, a big square, then a small square in a big square, then a big triangle, and expect me to find a small triangle in a big triangle. I have to say the words, describe what I'm seeing. If Tinker Mountain erupted, I'd be likely to notice. But if I want to notice the lesser cataclysms of valley life, I have to maintain in my head a running description of the present. It's not that I'm not observant; it's just that I talk too much.

Annie Dillard, *Pilgrim at Tinker Creek*

There is a quiet, delicate whisper that flutters in the center of our being. It is not the voice of reason or the voice of our parents telling us what to do. It is not the voice of the intellect or the voice of emotion. It is a gentle

whisper, an intuitive push, a yearning, a vision. Sometimes we pretend
not to hear, sometimes we try to listen but it is hard to discern from the
other chatter, and sometimes we simply try to silence it. But it will not
be silenced. It is the voice of your spirit that whispers messages of divine
guidance. It is trying to lead you to a life that has meaning and purpose
that is joyful. And the reason it is hard to hear and easy to ignore is
because we have been taught our entire life, indeed for centuries now,
not to heed that which is not rational, not conventional, not sane, not
ordinary, not profitable. But if ignored or muzzled, God simply gets
louder and louder until we must pay attention.

We don't want God yelling a divine plan.

בָּרוּךְ אַתָּה, יְיָ אֱלֹהֵינוּ, מֶלֶךְ הָעוֹלָם, אֲשֶׁר קִדְּשָׁנוּ
בְּמִצְוֹתָיו וְצִוָּנוּ עַל סְפִירַת הָעֹמֶר.

Baruch atah, Adonai Eloheinu, Melech haolam, asher kid'shanu
b'mitzvotav v'tzivanu al s'firat haomer.

Praised be You, Adonai our God, who rules the universe,
instilling within us the holiness of mitzvot by commanding us
to count the Omer.

Today is the twelfth day—one week and five days of the Omer.

13th Day of the Omer

We speak of genius when we speak of leadership, hoping for some of that elusive genius in ourselves, but the word *genius* in its Latin originality means simply, *the spirit of a place.* The genius of the Galapagos lies in its being unutterably itself; the genius of an individual lies in the inhabitation of their peculiar and particular spirit in conversation with the world. Genius is something that is itself and no other thing.

The task is simple and takes a life pilgrimage to attain, to inhabit our life fully, just as we find it, and in that inhabitation, let everything ripen to the next stage of conversation. . . . The cliff edge of mortality is very near. We must know how easy it is to forget, how easy it is to drift onto the rocks and put our lives to hazard. Everything is at stake, and everything in creation, if we are listening, is in conversation with us to tell us so.

David Whyte, *Crossing the Unknown Sea:*
Work as a Pilgrimage of Identity

There are times when you chase your destiny, and there are times when your destiny chases you. Pay attention: are you in pursuit or are you being pursued?

If you are being chased by your destiny, you will notice multiple forces converge, pushing you, pulling you. You will sense a synergy, a conspiracy of circumstance. Thought and coincidence will collide. Always follow the energy. Let it guide you, chart your direction, forge your path, inform your decisions.

When destiny pursues you, it is best to allow yourself to be caught, even if you do not completely understand.

בָּרוּךְ אַתָּה, יְיָ אֱלֹהֵינוּ, מֶלֶךְ הָעוֹלָם, אֲשֶׁר קִדְּשָׁנוּ בְּמִצְוֹתָיו וְצִוָּנוּ עַל סְפִירַת הָעֹמֶר.

Baruch atah, Adonai Eloheinu, Melech haolam, asher kid'shanu b'mitzvotav v'tzivanu al s'firat haomer.

Praised be You, Adonai our God, who rules the universe, instilling within us the holiness of mitzvot by commanding us to count the Omer.

Today is the thirteenth day—one week and six days of the Omer.

29   NISAN

14th Day of the Omer

"If you listen, listen to the voice of [Adonai] your God . . ." (Deuteronomy 28:1). The Midrash comments: "Happy is the one whose listenings are to Me, hovering always at My doorways, door within door. . . ."

"Listenings" means that one should always be prepared to receive and listen closely to the words of God. The voice of that word is in everything, since each was created by God's utterance and has the power of divine speech hidden within it. This is the hidden light that we are told to find.

Inwardness goes on, deeper and deeper, truly beyond measure. This is the meaning of "My doorways." Never think that you have come to the truth; understand that you are always standing at the entrance. The word "doorway" (*delet*) is related to "poverty" [or "humility"] (*dalut*). This is the way that you find door after door opening for you, [by always knowing how little you have achieved thus far].

The Language of Truth: The Torah Commentary
of the Sefat Emet, translated by Arthur Green

Be ready. When a moment of grace occurs and divine wisdom comes to you, you will be able to hear, and something within you will open— like a door. But you must always be standing at the threshold, that thin line between knowing and humility.

בָּרוּךְ אַתָּה, יְיָ אֱלֹהֵינוּ, מֶלֶךְ הָעוֹלָם, אֲשֶׁר קִדְּשָׁנוּ
בְּמִצְוֹתָיו וְצִוָּנוּ עַל סְפִירַת הָעֹמֶר.

Baruch atah, Adonai Eloheinu, Melech haolam, asher kid'shanu
b'mitzvotav v'tzivanu al s'firat haomer.

Praised be You, Adonai our God, who rules the universe,
instilling within us the holiness of mitzvot by commanding us
to count the Omer.

Today is the fourteenth day—two weeks of the Omer.

DISCERN

The Dove of Silence, I prayed:

Be gracious unto me
for I am surrounded by people who wish to consume me.

And then came the day when I was most afraid
and I put my trust in You.

When I surrender to faith,
fear steps aside and I fall silent.

What power do others truly have over my spirit?

Peace is like a dove, gracefully soaring,
silent, humble in beauty.

Help understand my path, to heed the callings
of my greatest potential.

Week Three:

Choose

And they encamped . . . at the edge

of the wilderness.

Exodus 13:20

Choosing is as continuous as living. Alongside the instincts of breathing and blinking and the beating of the heart is the very human imperative to choose. Daily, moment by moment, life is a sequence of choices. We choose to act or not, to react or not. What we believe, how we feel—boredom, passion, and kindness—don't merely happen to us; they are all choices we make.

In the geography of the soul, choice is a powerful spiritual principle. It enables us to assert control over things within our control. It enables us to understand how to relate to and dance with things not in our control. It fosters intentional living. And it draws a line in the sand, a boundary between what is in our control and what is not. This is an important boundary, a borderline that is drawn over and over as shifting sands blur. It is important to focus on choices we can make and learn not to lament the factors that are not in our control. Choosing is intentional living. Choosing is our ability to control and order our days. Not choosing throws us into the willy-nilly land of happenstance.

We all live at the edge of the wilderness, where we are just about to leave or just about to enter. And though the shortest distance between two points is a straight line, Moses walked a curve to redemption.

30 NISAN

15th Day of the Omer

Shekhinah [God's presence] does not reside except in a heart which is contrite. . . . A person must prepare a lovely dwelling place in his heart for the Shekhinah. This means that an individual has to act humbly and avoid losing his temper. For when he behaves in an arrogant manner, the Shekhinah takes flight and a handmaiden rules in her mistress' place.

Elijah de Vidas, in *Safed Spirituality: Rules of Mystical Piety,
The Beginning of Widsom,* translated by Laurence Fine

Demand of yourself and others graciousness and civil conversation. It really does matter.

בָּרוּךְ אַתָּה, יְיָ אֱלֹהֵינוּ, מֶלֶךְ הָעוֹלָם, אֲשֶׁר קִדְּשָׁנוּ
בְּמִצְוֹתָיו וְצִוָּנוּ עַל סְפִירַת הָעֹמֶר.

Baruch atah, Adonai Eloheinu, Melech haolam, asher kid'shanu
b'mitzvotav v'tzivanu al s'firat haomer.

Praised be You, Adonai our God, who rules the universe,
instilling within us the holiness of mitzvot by commanding us
to count the Omer.

Today is the fifteenth day—two weeks and one day of the Omer.

1 IYAR

16th Day of the Omer

Anger and tenderness: my selves.
And now I can believe they breathe in me
as angels, not polarities.
Anger and tenderness: the spider's genius
to spin and weave in the same action
from her own body, anywhere—
even from a broken web.

"Integrity" by Adrienne Rich,
in *A Wild Patience Has Taken Me This Far*

Be aware of fear. If it warns you of danger, take heed. Don't second-guess yourself.

But if it lives silently in your heart as a part of who you have become, it may lead you astray. In the world of the spirit, the opposite of love is not hate but rather it is fear. Fear of what? That love, abundant and free flowing, is somehow remote, far and inaccessible.

Here are the rules:

Do not permit your perceptions of what is true to be based on a
habit of fearful impulses.

Do not speak if there is fear in your heart. Your words will lack
   clarity and precision. They will not be wise nor will they be
   compassionate. Better to keep silent.
Do not allow your strategies, actions, or plans to be driven by fearful assumptions.

בָּרוּךְ אַתָּה, יְיָ אֱלֹהֵינוּ, מֶלֶךְ הָעוֹלָם, אֲשֶׁר קִדְּשָׁנוּ
בְּמִצְוֹתָיו וְצִוָּנוּ עַל סְפִירַת הָעֹמֶר.

Baruch atah, Adonai Eloheinu, Melech haolam, asher kid'shanu
b'mitzvotav v'tzivanu al s'firat haomer.

Praised be You, Adonai our God, who rules the universe,
instilling within us the holiness of mitzvot by commanding us
to count the Omer.

Today is the sixteenth day—two weeks and two days of the Omer.

2 IYAR

17th Day of the Omer

A person may come to sense two kinds of movement
    taking place within him during prayer.
At times you may feel the left hand of God
    pushing you away;
    at other times God's right hand draws you near.
But even as you are pushed away,
    know still
    that this is only for the sake of your return.
Even as you feel
    the might of God's left hand upon you,
    see that it is God Himself
    who touches you.
This too accept in love,
    and, trembling, kiss the hand that pushes you—
    for in that very moment,
    the right hand awaits your coming near.

Your Word Is Fire: The Hasidic Masters on Contemplative Prayer, edited and
translated by Rabbi Arthur Green and Dr. Barry W. Holtz

Standing at the trailhead of Taggert Lake in the Grand Teton National Park, we had to choose left or right. We went left, just because, or so I thought. We walked along the wooded path, my eyes cast downward. Each step was soft against the damp earth and every heartbeat hard against my chest. The hike was a bit hard for me. Ezra, on the other hand, ran ahead, quick and light like an exuberant child on a playground. I was deep in thought, waiting for God to sigh, or laugh or just whisper to my heart. I could smell the sage from the mountains above and the mist and the forest and then . . . a sound. Not wind, not animal, not human. A creak or maybe a groaning sound, like a violin bow against a single string on the lowest possible register. I stood still, quiet, so that my breath could not be confused with the noise in the woods. There it was again. I looked up and saw a tree thick at the base and separated into two thin trunks as they reached high, very high, into the sky. They were swaying against the wind. And as the wind blew, the tree had no choice but to yield, and yield again, back and forth, creaking, groaning, resisting, yielding.

I called to Ezra and we stood awhile eavesdropping on their conversation—tree against wind, wind against tree, resisting, yielding. And I knew that God had spoken. And I realized that to live deeply and at one with life's purpose would require a yielding of sorts. It's all a dance between resistance and giving way. Whatever resistance I feel, whatever my fears and hurt, my insecurities and pain, they all need to bend to the forces of love, and hope, and faith. All will be as it should. Life teaches through harshness and softness. We are summoned to live a better and lovelier life; calmer, quieter, more aware. And even when it is hard, and we can feel the exertion of the beating of our heart, we must yield to as much kindness as humanly possible. On that day in the woods, the stiffness of my spirit began to yield against the breath of God.

בָּרוּךְ אַתָּה, יְיָ אֱלֹהֵינוּ, מֶלֶךְ הָעוֹלָם, אֲשֶׁר קִדְּשָׁנוּ
בְּמִצְוֹתָיו וְצִוָּנוּ עַל סְפִירַת הָעֹמֶר.

Baruch atah, Adonai Eloheinu, Melech haolam, asher kid'shanu
b'mitzvotav v'tzivanu al s'firat haomer.

Praised be You, Adonai our God, who rules the universe,
instilling within us the holiness of mitzvot by commanding us
to count the Omer.

Today is the seventeenth day—two weeks and three days of
the·Omer.

Raise me upon a rock...

lead me on a level path...

that I might enjoy the goodness of God,

in the land of the living.

PSALM 27:5, 27:11, 27:13

3   IYAR

18th Day of the Omer

During my early adult years, my fight with God reached its peak. My ego convinced me that the world was a most painful place, and I became increasingly preoccupied with my fear of rejection. My way of life, as I followed my fragmented and often conflicted roadmap, continued to illustrate the truth that *you get what you expect.* I fully believed that if something bad was going to happen to someone, I would be that someone.

Although part of me rejected God, another part of my mind felt that God was punishing me for all my misdeeds. I also believed that I was being punished for things I didn't even know I had done. . . .

The simplicity of choosing to live a life of love, rather than a life of fear, is more clearly becoming a reality for me. The power of simply remembering God, and remembering that my true identity is love, has been beyond anything I could have imagined.

Gerald G. Jampolsky, MD, *Out of Darkness into the Light:*
A Journey of Inner Healing

When the circumstances of our life become dramatic, out of control, maddening, unpleasant, that may be a sign to live another way, to choose something different, to change direction.

Sometimes what seems irrational is right.

Sometimes what seems unconventional is creative, groundbreaking.

And sometimes what seems insane is clarity; pure and sacred light.

בָּרוּךְ אַתָּה, יְיָ אֱלֹהֵינוּ, מֶלֶךְ הָעוֹלָם, אֲשֶׁר קִדְּשָׁנוּ
בְּמִצְוֹתָיו וְצִוָּנוּ עַל סְפִירַת הָעֹמֶר.

*Baruch atah, Adonai Eloheinu, Melech haolam, asher kid'shanu
b'mitzvotav v'tzivanu al s'firat haomer.*

Praised be You, Adonai our God, who rules the universe,
instilling within us the holiness of mitzvot by commanding us
to count the Omer.

Today is the eighteenth day—two weeks and four days of the Omer.

4   IYAR

19th Day of the Omer

"In the World to Come," taught Rabbi Zusya of Hanipol, "they will not ask me: 'Why were you not more like Moses our teacher?' They will ask: 'Why were you not more like Zusya?'"

The Classic Tales: 4000 Years of Jewish Lore,
edited by Ellen Frankel

Do you remember your childhood daydreams? When you imagined yourself all grown up, who were you to become? When you played alone, what was your favorite game? When you were young, what was your favorite nighttime dream?

Do you remember feeling free?

If you were to adjust your life, aligning it with your dreams, what would be your next step in becoming who you were always meant to be?

בָּרוּךְ אַתָּה, יְיָ אֱלֹהֵינוּ, מֶלֶךְ הָעוֹלָם, אֲשֶׁר קִדְּשָׁנוּ
בְּמִצְוֹתָיו וְצִוָּנוּ עַל סְפִירַת הָעֹמֶר.

*Baruch atah, Adonai Eloheinu, Melech haolam, asher kid'shanu
b'mitzvotav v'tzivanu al s'firat haomer.*

Praised be You, Adonai our God, who rules the universe,
instilling within us the holiness of mitzvot by commanding us
to count the Omer.

Today is the nineteenth day—two weeks and five days of the Omer.

5 IYAR

20th Day of the Omer

Someone spoke to me last night,
told me the truth. Just a few words,
but I recognized it.
I knew I should make myself get up,
write it down, but it was late,
and I was exhausted from working
all day in the garden, moving rocks.
Now, I remember only the flavor—
not like food, sweet or sharp.
More like a fine powder, like dust.
And I wasn't elated or frightened,
but simply rapt, aware.
That's how it is sometimes—
God comes to your window,
all bright light and black wings,
and you're just too tired to open it.

"Dust" by Dorianne Laux, in *What We Carry*

I wonder how it would be if I answered the call, if I allowed myself to hear the call, if I believed that I was called? Out of the confusion, clarity; out of the daze, wonder; out of the mundane, purpose; out of the darkness, light.

And now the morning light falls upon the trees. And the leaves toward the east are illuminated. Those leaves that face west wait patiently.

בָּרוּךְ אַתָּה, יְיָ אֱלֹהֵינוּ, מֶלֶךְ הָעוֹלָם, אֲשֶׁר קִדְּשָׁנוּ בְּמִצְוֹתָיו וְצִוָּנוּ עַל סְפִירַת הָעֹמֶר.

Baruch atah, Adonai Eloheinu, Melech haolam, asher kid'shanu b'mitzvotav v'tzivanu al s'firat haomer.

Praised be You, Adonai our God, who rules the universe, instilling within us the holiness of mitzvot by commanding us to count the Omer.

Today is the twentieth day—two weeks and six days of the Omer.

This is the purpose of our creation:

That each find the place in which we belong.

ADAPTED FROM S'FAT EMET, *VAYEITZEI*

6 IYAR

21st Day of the Omer

We find in the fields of Nature no place that is blank or barren; every spot on land or sea is covered with harvests, and these harvests are always ripe and ready to be gathered, and no toiler is ever underpaid. Not in these fields, God's wilds, will you ever hear the sad moan of disappointment, "All is vanity." No, we are overpaid a thousand times for all our toil, and a single day in so divine an atmosphere of beauty and love would be well worth living for, and at its close, should death come, without any hope of another life, we could still say, "Thank you, God, for the glorious gift!" and pass on. Indeed, some of the days I have spent alone in the depths of the wilderness have shown me that immortal life beyond the grave is not essential to perfect happiness, for these diverse days were so complete there was no sense of time in them, they had no definite beginning or ending, and formed a kind of terrestrial immortality. After days like these we are ready for any fate—pain, grief, death or oblivion—with grateful heart for the glorious gift as long as hearts shall endure. In the meantime, our indebtedness is growing ever more. The sun shines and the stars, and new beauty meets us at every step in all our wanderings.

Meditations of John Muir: Nature's Temple,
edited by Chris Highland

Examine your life with care and compassion. And honesty. Notice the negativity that surrounds you. The relationships that do not support you. The behaviors that are obstacles in your path.

Now ask—in what way are these people and behaviors serving you?

Sometimes we hold tight to negative patterns because there is something we need to learn or because we think they keep us safe or because it's the only way we've known or because we do not yet understand the power we have to choose differently.

Know this, as long as behaviors, patterns, and relationships serve you, you will keep them in your life. But if they no longer serve you, you are free, absolutely free, to choose another way.

בָּרוּךְ אַתָּה, יְיָ אֱלֹהֵינוּ, מֶלֶךְ הָעוֹלָם, אֲשֶׁר קִדְּשָׁנוּ בְּמִצְוֺתָיו וְצִוָּנוּ עַל סְפִירַת הָעֹמֶר.

Baruch atah, Adonai Eloheinu, Melech haolam, asher ḳid'shanu b'mitzvotav v'tzivanu al s'firat haomer.

Praised be You, Adonai our God, who rules the universe, instilling within us the holiness of mitzvot by commanding us to count the Omer.

Today is the twenty-first day—three weeks of the Omer.

CHOOSE

Dearest God,
Creator of light,
You set before me
blessing, life, goodness.

Guide me, comfort me.

Through my longing,
gently urge me to find my life's purpose.

Like the grasses of the field
bend to the wind
I bow, humble.
I choose life.

Week Four:

Hope

And God said, *I will take you out*
of the misery of Egypt.

Exodus 3:17

I t is possible to gaze upon the horizon and see that it is far away, distant from your touch, and it is, in essence, an illusion. A mirage. The thin boundary between heaven and earth shifts and changes and morphs, and it is simply not real. And in your heart you say, *how impossible to catch the beauty in the distance* and quickly turn away, eyes cast down to the smallness of now. And in this moment you are susceptible to cynicism or indifference or both.

And it is possible to gaze upon the horizon and see its vastness as abundance and possibility. That thin line between heaven and earth is a reminder that your reach can extend beyond this simple life of circumstance and happenstance. And you gaze upon the horizon and you are inspired, and enlivened and hopeful. Hope is anticipation, and anticipation is invigorating.

And when you gaze upon the horizon and extend your hand to touch its magnificence, your mind expands and your heart knows joy and your spirit believes in the beauty that it sees. And you believe in the human capacity for change. You believe in the children. You believe that despite your current circumstance, things can be better. You believe with the strength of your character and with determination, you can mend what is broken.

When you gaze upon the horizon and take a breath, catch your breath, and realize that you can live with light and goodness.

Do not look away. Practice hope. And when you do, you practice gratitude.

7 IYAR

22nd Day of the Omer

The life of spirit ebbs and flows. There are times in our lives when we are open to religious experience, when we are ripe to find connection, meaning, in every stream of sunlight, in the sight of winter birds coming into formation, catching a glimpse of a now-grown daughter asleep, your eyes suddenly able to peel back the years to the child's face underneath. A hundred possibilities in nature and in human meeting. Every few days we seem to have another encounter with some new person in which we feel what is holy passing between us. Maybe those are the experiences we call Sinai.

Merle Feld, *A Spiritual Life: A Jewish Feminist Journey*

We say in our prayers: God sustains the world with grace.

In Hebrew the word for "sustain," *m'chalkeil,* is rooted in the word "everything," *kol,* and related to the word "vessel," *k'li.*

How beautiful the metaphor! How affirming the prayer . . .

The world is a crafted vessel, made of light, overflowing with grace, abundantly sustained, by God.

And you, and you.

בָּרוּךְ אַתָּה, יְיָ אֱלֹהֵינוּ, מֶלֶךְ הָעוֹלָם, אֲשֶׁר קִדְּשָׁנוּ
בְּמִצְוֹתָיו וְצִוָּנוּ עַל סְפִירַת הָעֹמֶר.

Baruch atah, Adonai Eloheinu, Melech haolam, asher kid'shanu
b'mitzvotav v'tzivanu al s'firat haomer.

Praised be You, Adonai our God, who rules the universe,
instilling within us the holiness of mitzvot by commanding us
to count the Omer.

Today is the twenty-second day—three weeks and one day of
the Omer.

8   IYAR

23rd Day of the Omer

No one ever told me the coming of the Messiah
Could be an inward thing;
No one ever told me a change of heart
Might be as quiet as new-fallen snow.

No one ever told me that redemption
Was as simple as springtime and as wonderful
As birds returning after a long winter,
Rose-breasted grosbeaks singing in the swaying branches
Of a newly budded tree.

No one ever told me that salvation
Might be like a fresh spring wind
Blowing away the dried withered leaves of another year,
Carrying the scent of flowers, the promise of fruition.

What I found for myself I try to tell you:
Redemption and salvation are very near,
And the taste of them is in the world
That God created and laid before us.

"Discovery" by Ruth F. Brin,
in *Harvest: Collected Poems and Prayers*

Everything passes. Moments pass. Moments of crisis and moments of calm all pass.

Life is a force; it flows with breath and energy, desire and need, hunger and pain, peace and belonging, knowing and doubt. Like the wind, like the scorching summer, like the bitterness of coffee, like the orange of a late-day moon, like the radiance of trees in the spring, like the high-pitched cry of your firstborn baby, like the beauty of your youth, like the whispers of midnight.

Everything passes.

And yet, the strength of your character, the nature of your relationships, and the depth of love in your life all linger in the air; like the transcendent energy that is neither created nor destroyed.

בָּרוּךְ אַתָּה, יְיָ אֱלֹהֵינוּ, מֶלֶךְ הָעוֹלָם, אֲשֶׁר קִדְּשָׁנוּ בְּמִצְוֹתָיו וְצִוָּנוּ עַל סְפִירַת הָעֹמֶר.

Baruch atah, Adonai Eloheinu, Melech haolam, asher kid'shanu
b'mitzvotav v'tzivanu al s'firat haomer.

Praised be You, Adonai our God, who rules the universe,
instilling within us the holiness of mitzvot by commanding us
to count the Omer.

Today is the twenty-third day—three weeks and two days of
the Omer.

Those who trust in God
shall renew their strength;
they shall rise up with wings as eagles;
they shall run, and not be weary;
and they shall walk, and not faint.

Isaiah 40:31

24th Day of the Omer

Rebbe Menahem Mendel of Kotsk once asked his followers where God was. "Everywhere of course," they retorted, shocked that their teacher should even pose so elementary a question. "No," he replied, "God is where we let God in." As we create space inside ourselves, God is able to descend to meet us there. If we are full up with ourselves, how can God get in? Of course, we shouldn't expect a great revelation, but every life has its moments. God is there behind our clouds, descends into our heart, meets us in a word, in a fine morning, in some inconspicuous act of kindness. It could be anything, anywhere.

Jonathan Wittenberg,
The Eternal Journey: Meditations on the Jewish Year

Chatter is all around us. People talking about politics and war; children and spouses; dinner plans and lunch dates; television shows and celebrity gossip; basketball, soccer, hockey, and football; ways to make money and office politics. We fill the silences with conversations. Some that matter and many that don't.

Once, I was sitting in prayer and I listened to voices chanting an ancient chorus. I was transported by the sound and felt as if I was eavesdropping on whispers behind some mysterious curtain:

The angels turn to one another and ask,
"Where is the place of God?"
They call out in song and answer one to the other,
"God is in God's place."

And so, perhaps the spiritual journey is a simple reconciliation between what appears to be mundane and what seems to be extraordinary. That is to say, if we live an ordinary life of simple chatter and routine acts, what a difference it would make to see within those moments light, hope, miracle, joy, holiness.

There is the possibility of the sacred in every place we ask the question: God, where are You?

בָּרוּךְ אַתָּה, יְיָ אֱלֹהֵינוּ, מֶלֶךְ הָעוֹלָם, אֲשֶׁר קִדְּשָׁנוּ
בְּמִצְוֹתָיו וְצִוָּנוּ עַל סְפִירַת הָעֹמֶר.

*Baruch atah, Adonai Eloheinu, Melech haolam, asher kid'shanu
b'mitzvotav v'tzivanu al s'firat haomer.*

Praised be You, Adonai our God, who rules the universe,
instilling within us the holiness of mitzvot by commanding us
to count the Omer.

Today is the twenty-fourth day—three weeks and three days
of the Omer.

25th Day of the Omer

The bud
stands for all things,
even for those things that don't flower,
 for everything flowers, from within, of self-blessing;
though sometimes it is necessary
to reteach a thing its loveliness,
to put a hand on the brow
of the flower
and retell it in words and in touch
it is lovely
until it flowers again from within, of self-blessing.

"Saint Francis and the Sow"
by Galway Kinnell, in *Three Books*

The human spirit has infinite capacity. We can hold within us a paradox. We can experience both joy and sadness. The joy does not diminish the loss; the loss does not diminish the joy.

Sometimes we live as if we need to make a choice between positive and negative emotions, as if to choose one is to betray the other. We seem to say, how can I be happy when I have the sadness of loss, when I live with uncertainty, when a loved one is suffering, when the world is suffering? Or, we say, how can I live in sadness when there is so much to be grateful for, so many blessings, so much reason for gladness?

And sometimes we live as if we are in competition for the attention and admiration of others. We want them to choose us, to love us, to pay attention to us. But people have an infinite capacity to love, if they are not made to choose. We can love completely and utterly, so much, so many.

The human spirit has infinite capacity to feel all things, to live as if all is possible, to love, to imagine, to experience, to hope, to rise above. This is the meaning of abundance.

בָּרוּךְ אַתָּה, יְיָ אֱלֹהֵינוּ, מֶלֶךְ הָעוֹלָם, אֲשֶׁר קִדְּשָׁנוּ בְּמִצְוֹתָיו וְצִוָּנוּ עַל סְפִירַת הָעֹמֶר.

Baruch atah, Adonai Eloheinu, Melech haolam, asher ḳid'shanu b'mitzvotav v'tzivanu al s'firat haomer.

Praised be You, Adonai our God, who rules the universe, instilling within us the holiness of mitzvot by commanding us to count the Omer.

Today is the twenty-fifth day—three weeks and four days of the Omer.

Majestic is the presence of God throughout.
You have covered the heavens with splendor.

Psalm 8:2

26th Day of the Omer

The joy, the triumph, the delight, the madness,
The boundless, overflowing, bursting gladness,
The vaporous exultation not to be confined!
Ha! Ha! The animation of delight
Which wraps me, like an atmosphere of light,
And bears me as a cloud is borne by its own wind!

Percy Bysshe Shelley, *Prometheus Unbound*, act 4

It is cold at the cemetery. I think that the wind must feel the sorrow. Sitting on folding chairs, the family is stunned.

The son said, "It's not like we didn't know that this day would come. Dad was in his eighties, ailing. It's just that I never imagined myself as . . . fatherless." The grave is open. The casket sways as a strong breeze goes by. Tears seem to be stuck in the rim of his eyes.

I whisper to the family, though everyone who is there can hear, "You know, it is traditional at the graveside, moments before the burial to silently contemplate forgiveness. Ask for forgiveness and you, in turn, accept your father's unspoken request for forgiveness. All people are frail. All relationships are flawed. Love and hurt are so intertwined that sometimes you cannot see the difference. Say you're sorry. Say it's OK."

"How can I say I am sorry to the dead?"

"How can you not?"

"How can I forgive him?"

"How can you not? Here. Offer a prayer of forgiveness. Your life depends on it. Open up your hand as I place the sandy-colored earth from the Land of Israel in your palm. Feel its texture, its power. What passes through your heart at this moment is both private and universal. The earth in your hand teaches us that grief, love, and loss are shared throughout time and place. Let the earth fall onto the coffin; let it be taken by the wind. See it fly away with the spirit of all that is good in life. See it fall onto the ground, onto the casket. See it return to the earth from where it came."

In the end, what passes turns to dust and what is essential is eternal.

בָּרוּךְ אַתָּה, יְיָ אֱלֹהֵינוּ, מֶלֶךְ הָעוֹלָם, אֲשֶׁר קִדְּשָׁנוּ בְּמִצְוֹתָיו וְצִוָּנוּ עַל סְפִירַת הָעֹמֶר.

Baruch atah, Adonai Eloheinu, Melech haolam, asher kid'shanu b'mitzvotav v'tzivanu al s'firat haomer.

Praised be You, Adonai our God, who rules the universe, instilling within us the holiness of mitzvot by commanding us to count the Omer.

Today is the twenty-sixth day—three weeks and five days of the Omer.

12   IYAR

27th Day of the Omer

Today, like every other day, we wake up empty
and frightened. Don't open the door to the study
and begin reading. Take down a musical instrument.

Let the beauty we love be what we do.
There are hundreds of ways to kneel and kiss the ground.

"Let the Beauty We Love,"
in *A Year with Rumi: Daily Readings*,
translated by Coleman Barks

Sometimes we are unable to believe that change is possible.

Take one courageous step, today.
Do something kind for someone, today.

This is a prayer of simplicity, yet its power is as solid as the ground beneath your feet.
And as sacred.

בָּרוּךְ אַתָּה, יְיָ אֱלֹהֵינוּ, מֶלֶךְ הָעוֹלָם, אֲשֶׁר קִדְּשָׁנוּ
בְּמִצְוֹתָיו וְצִוָּנוּ עַל סְפִירַת הָעֹמֶר.

Baruch atah, Adonai Eloheinu, Melech haolam, asher kid'shanu
b'mitzvotav v'tzivanu al s'firat haomer.

Praised be You, Adonai our God, who rules the universe,
instilling within us the holiness of mitzvot by commanding us
to count the Omer.

Today is the twenty-seventh day—three weeks and six days of
the Omer.

13   IYAR

28th Day of the Omer

The eye has a dark part and a light part. One can see only through the dark part.

Midrash Tanchuma, Parashat T'tzaveh

Once I went to the mountains to find God in the mist. How perfect it was that I arrived in the darkness, the mountains hidden behind the mask of night. And I walked from the small plane and felt the cold air, sharp like a slap. I of course was startled. And the million stars laughed at my foolishness. And I did not need to wait for the dawn and the morning mist, because though the darkness was absolute, so was my capacity to see. And I suddenly witnessed a shift, a great willingness to be carried away from my busy-disinterested-uninspired self. And before I even left the tarmac to claim my luggage, I had all that I needed.

בָּרוּךְ אַתָּה, יְיָ אֱלֹהֵינוּ, מֶלֶךְ הָעוֹלָם, אֲשֶׁר קִדְּשָׁנוּ
בְּמִצְוֹתָיו וְצִוָּנוּ עַל סְפִירַת הָעֹמֶר.

Baruch atah, Adonai Eloheinu, Melech haolam, asher ḳid'shanu
b'mitzvotav v'tzivanu al s'firat haomer.

Praised be You, Adonai our God, who rules the universe,
instilling within us the holiness of mitzvot by commanding us
to count the Omer.

Today is the twenty-eighth day—four weeks of the Omer.

HOPE

Creator of darkness and light,
banish my despair,
turn aside my indifference,
soften the callousness of my heart.

Open my eyes
that I may see that
beauty abounds,
and that love abides.

Enlighten my life with
holiness and grace.
As it is written:
Come, let us walk in the light of God (Isaiah 2:5).

Week Five:

Imagine

And God said, *I will take you* . . .
to a land flowing with milk and honey.

Exodus 3:17

God declared that the land was flowing with milk and honey. But it was not. The land had date palms, tall, ready to yield their fruit that could become honey. And it had goats grazing peacefully on the side of mountains, ready to give milk. And we bless God who brings forth bread from the earth. But God does not. Rather, the fields are abundant with golden grain, waiting for harvest, waiting for human endeavor. The sustenance from milk, the satisfaction from bread, the sweetness of honey all require us to see what is, imagine what could be, and create what we can.

This is the secret of our power: To see the invisible! To pull back the veil that obscures all that is good. To bear witness to what is possible despite what others believe is merely probable. To look at what is and see what could be. To see the path to hope, courage, meaning, and purpose.

Magnificence is possible, and joy is possible.

This is the secret of our power: To imagine! And then to create! To step out of the darkness that blinds us to possibility. To see that our accomplishments begin with potential, with an idea, with thought. To envision ourselves as capable of so much more. To behold and then to make manifest.

Blessed be your basket
and your kneading bowl.

DEUTERONOMY 28:5

14   IYAR

29th Day of the Omer

Outside my window, out over the Hudson, a very large bird is soaring. I have seen this bird for days now, sailing, sailing on the fierce winds that are the slipstream around this island. It is too large to be a hawk. It is not shaped like a gull. The Hudson Valley is full of eagles, higher up. I cannot believe this is one, but it seems to know exactly what it is: eagle. It doesn't tell its name. It wears it. Maybe . . . we are such birds, mistaken by ourselves and others for something else, riding the current of our dreams, hunting in the canyons of commerce for something we have seen from higher up.

Julia Cameron, *The Artist's Way:*
A Spiritual Path to Higher Creativity

Perhaps the greatest sin of our teachers was the command to stop daydreaming. I am sure that they didn't mean to be so harsh. But for some, a door closed, hinges rusted shut, and even now, there is no air inside.

I remember my defiance so well. I would take the thick leaded pencil in my hand and press it against the wide blues lines of tan pages. I was supposed to be practicing my handwriting, but I was not. I was watching the lines form and dance before my eyes as I imagined words alive with thought and thought filled with images and images packed with meaning and meaning revealing the great secrets of the universe. And though I was eight or so, and wouldn't have said it quite that way, I knew that daydreaming was the key to my survival and the abracadabra of my success.

בָּרוּךְ אַתָּה, יְיָ אֱלֹהֵינוּ, מֶלֶךְ הָעוֹלָם, אֲשֶׁר קִדְּשָׁנוּ בְּמִצְוֹתָיו וְצִוָּנוּ עַל סְפִירַת הָעֹמֶר.

Baruch atah, Adonai Eloheinu, Melech haolam, asher kid'shanu b'mitzvotav v'tzivanu al s'firat haomer.

Praised be You, Adonai our God, who rules the universe, instilling within us the holiness of mitzvot by commanding us to count the Omer.

Today is the twenty-ninth day—four weeks and one day of the Omer.

15   IYAR

30th Day of the Omer

There is something in life more important, more beautiful, and more satisfying than what we "think" is important. That "something" is an internal place beyond thought, beyond form. Our thoughts about what we want, what we wish were different, and where we would rather be will come and go. But behind these thoughts, before their very formation, a deeper level of life is waiting for our attention. This is the realm of the Soul. The Soul is the part of us that watches our thoughts come and go. It is not thoughts themselves.

For most of us—certainly for me—thoughts are extremely compelling. . . . We think; we feel; then we think some more. We want to believe that if we could just think through our dissatisfactions or analyze our problems, we would somehow feel better. But that never works, because nourishment for the Soul comes not from the intellect but from the heart. We can't think our way to happiness. Instead, we must open ourselves to our true nature, which *is* happiness.

Richard Carlson, in *Handbook for the Soul,*
edited by Richard Carlson and Benjamin Shield

The path was an incline, rocky, a bit hard to navigate. It was made harder by a swarm of grasshoppers. They jumped and flew around my ankles and calves, bumping into me, scratchy and annoying. But this was their path, and there was no way to fight it. So I paused a moment and I listened. They were yellow, two to three inches long. And they were busy, a colony of vibration jumping in delight. And then I heard them, a clatter of sound like the Mormon Tabernacle choir, a vibrant song unto God. And I looked up and between the mountains, distant from the path, was a clearing, a field. It too seemed alive, silently vibrating with shimmers of light. I squinted, thinking it was a mirage—the way heat looks like waves off a hood of a hot car. But no, it was the small leaves of the trees. They seemed to clutch the wind and the light and were dancing, unabashed, thinking no one was there to see.

But there I was, called upon to be a testifying witness.

So I swear to the holy presence of music and splendor and to the capacity of the soul to see and hear what is often invisible and silent, the universe alive with grandeur.

בָּרוּךְ אַתָּה, יְיָ אֱלֹהֵינוּ, מֶלֶךְ הָעוֹלָם, אֲשֶׁר קִדְּשָׁנוּ בְּמִצְוֹתָיו וְצִוָּנוּ עַל סְפִירַת הָעֹמֶר.

Baruch atah, Adonai Eloheinu, Melech haolam, asher kid'shanu b'mitzvotav v'tzivanu al s'firat haomer.

Praised be You, Adonai our God, who rules the universe, instilling within us the holiness of mitzvot by commanding us to count the Omer.

Today is the thirtieth day—four weeks and two days of the Omer.

6   IYAR

31st Day of the Omer

Earth's crammed with heaven,
And every common bush afire with God:
But only he who sees, takes off his shoes,
The rest sit round it and pluck blackberries.

Elizabeth Barrett Browning, *Aurora Leigh*, book 7

In awe we stand before God's creation and the power of life! And yet, at times we feel vulnerable and exposed, and the exclamation point becomes a question mark. When we feel small, we ask how it all fits together. Life can be so big, so utterly overwhelming, and we are so very small. Awe turns to fear.

Go out into nature. Get up from your desk, from your easy chair, and venture into the woods, onto the shores of the lake, into the field, step onto any path. Stand among the shadows; turn your face toward the light. It is comforting not to be in the center of the universe. When the world revolves around us, the weight and pressure are too great. Fear causes us to hold tight to maintain control. But to be in the center is to be in a lonely place, and in truth, it is illusion, for we are never in the center.

I long to be a particle in a spray of light. I pray that I am one small part in a grander scheme. Standing in the majesty of nature I proclaim: How magnificent is life! How mysterious! And behold, upon the soft ground, patches of sun dance, and I say "amen."

בָּרוּךְ אַתָּה, יְיָ אֱלֹהֵינוּ, מֶלֶךְ הָעוֹלָם, אֲשֶׁר קִדְּשָׁנוּ בְּמִצְוֹתָיו וְצִוָּנוּ עַל סְפִירַת הָעֹמֶר.

Baruch atah, Adonai Eloheinu, Melech haolam, asher kid'shanu b'mitzvotav v'tzivanu al s'firat haomer.

Praised be You, Adonai our God, who rules the universe, instilling within us the holiness of mitzvot by commanding us to count the Omer.

Today is the thirty-first day—four weeks and three days of the Omer.

For you shall go out with joy,
and be led forth with peace:
the mountains and the hills
shall break forth before you into singing,
and all the trees of the field
shall clap their hands.

Isaiah 55:12

17   IYAR

32nd Day of the Omer

There are trees on the coast stripped of bark, stark silver white, and without the bark one can see how this very wood is twisted so the dead tree seems to be like a corkscrew rooted in the earth. There are people who think that only people have emotions like pride, fear, and joy, but those who know will tell you all things are alive, perhaps not in the same way we are alive, but each in its own way, as should be, for we are not all the same. And though different from us in shape and life span, different in Time and Knowing, yet are trees alive. And rocks. And water. And all know emotion.

Anne Cameron, *Daughters of Copper Woman*

Our life is a story of friendship and of loneliness, of love's complexities, of disappointments and betrayals. Of joy and success. A story where dreams wrestle with fear, where sustained boredom threatens our balance, and where wonder elevates our life.

All this and more make up a life and are the elements of a good story. The way in which we imagine the past directly informs the present. How do you see what was, how do you connect the events in your life? Are you victim? Are you hero? Do you learn from struggle or did your struggles defeat you?

When you speak of yourself, use words that are gentle, passionate. Speak of love, of courage, of perseverance, of strength of character, of fortitude.

And then, become the words you speak.

Become a beacon of light through which hope lights the way.

בָּרוּךְ אַתָּה, יְיָ אֱלֹהֵינוּ, מֶלֶךְ הָעוֹלָם, אֲשֶׁר קִדְּשָׁנוּ בְּמִצְוֹתָיו וְצִוָּנוּ עַל סְפִירַת הָעֹמֶר.

Baruch atah, Adonai Eloheinu, Melech haolam, asher kid'shanu b'mitzvotav v'tzivanu al s'firat haomer.

Praised be You, Adonai our God, who rules the universe, instilling within us the holiness of mitzvot by commanding us to count the Omer.

Today is the thirty-second day—four weeks and four days of the Omer.

18 IYAR

33rd Day of the Omer

The perception of the glory is a rare occurrence in our lives. We fail to wonder, we fail to respond to the presence. This is the tragedy of every man: "to dim all wonder by indifference." Life is routine, and routine is resistance to the wonder. "Replete is the world with a spiritual radiance, replete with sublime and marvelous secrets. But a small hand held against the eye hides it all," said the Baal Shem. "Just as a small coin held over the face can block out the sight of a mountain, so can the vanities of living block out the sight of the infinite light."

The wonders are daily with us, and yet "the miracle is not recognized by him who experiences it." Its apprehension is not a matter of physical perception. "Of what avail is an open eye, if the heart is blind?" One may see many things without observing them—"his ears are open, but he does not hear."

Rabbi Abraham Joshua Heschel, *God in Search of Man*

If your children have been diagnosed with learning differences, teach them the power of seeing things another way. Tell them that the world craves a unique perspective and that advancement depends on a creative and unconventional mind.

And if they are ordinary, tell them that there is nothing more ordinary than a field of wildflowers blooming in early spring. Tell them that they are a beautiful miracle that unfolds with majesty and grace. Teach them to hold daily moments as sacred, just as they are sacred.

And if you have children who are shy and quiet, tell them to listen to the heartbeat of the world, for only in silences can God's secrets be revealed. Show them the power of listening, and tell them that the people in their life will be grateful to them, for the quiet ones listen and people need to be heard.

And if your child is just a kid, eating a bit too many cookies, getting dirty when they should be clean, doing homework only sometimes, almost always preferring to play with friends, then learn from them. For we take life too seriously. Fun and laughter open our hearts to living.

Our greatest gift to our children is our delight in their precious lives. We must love them as they are, without the chaos caused by criticism and fear. We need only to encourage them, to love them, to keep them safe. Let all children grow up to become who they were born to be.

בָּרוּךְ אַתָּה, יְיָ אֱלֹהֵינוּ, מֶלֶךְ הָעוֹלָם, אֲשֶׁר קִדְּשָׁנוּ
בְּמִצְוֹתָיו וְצִוָּנוּ עַל סְפִירַת הָעֹמֶר.

*Baruch atah, Adonai Eloheinu, Melech haolam, asher kid'shanu
b'mitzvotav v'tzivanu al s'firat haomer.*

Praised be You, Adonai our God, who rules the universe,
instilling within us the holiness of mitzvot by commanding us
to count the Omer.

Today is the thirty-third day—four weeks and five days of the
Omer.

19   IYAR

34th Day of the Omer

And I have felt
A presence that disturbs me with joy
Of elevated thoughts; a sense of sublime
Of something far more deeply interfused,
Whose dwelling is the light of setting suns,
And the round ocean and the living air,
And the blue sky, and in the mind of man;
A motion and a spirit, that impels
All thinking things, all objects of all thought,
And rolls through all things.

William Wordsworth, "Lines Composed
a Few Miles above Tintern Abbey"

Angels fell to earth this week. I saw them as a dense thick fog, hovering, blocking the distance before me, and limiting my visibility. That's how I knew they were angels: they made me focus on what was right in front of me, and I became acutely aware of having impaired vision.

Sometimes angels fall to earth and we squint into the cloud to discern some eternal message of hope and resilience. The Torah says that when we wander in the wilderness we are to follow a cloud by day and a pillar of fire by night (Exodus 13:21). Because when we follow traces of God's presence, well, we call that guidance. But sometimes, we are taught, the cloud descends upon us and we cannot see ahead of us, no horizon to walk toward, no path to follow.

And when that happens, when the cloud descends and we are in a fog, that's when it's best not to journey. We camp and simply wait until it lifts. The waiting becomes imagining, envisioning the person we want to become, the paths of our complicated and twisting road.

And then, the Torah teaches, we know that God is in the cloud.

בָּרוּךְ אַתָּה, יְיָ אֱלֹהֵינוּ, מֶלֶךְ הָעוֹלָם, אֲשֶׁר קִדְּשָׁנוּ בְּמִצְוֹתָיו וְצִוָּנוּ עַל סְפִירַת הָעֹמֶר.

Baruch atah, Adonai Eloheinu, Melech haolam, asher kid'shanu b'mitzvotav v'tzivanu al s'firat haomer.

Praised be You, Adonai our God, who rules the universe, instilling within us the holiness of mitzvot by commanding us to count the Omer.

Today is the thirty-fourth day—four weeks and six days of the Omer.

20   IYAR

35th Day of the Omer

We mistake detail for being picayune or only for writing about ants and bobby pins. We think of detail as small, not the realm of the cosmic mind or these big hills of New Mexico. That isn't true. No matter how large a thing is, how fantastic, it is also ordinary. We think of details as daily and mundane. Even miracles are mundane happenings that an awakened mind can see in a fantastic way.

Natalie Goldberg, *Writing Down the Bones*

We live one small moment at a time. One breath, one glance, one thought at a time.

And yet, doesn't life feel like a freight train, a long deafening, fast blur? Is it trite to say that you are the conductor and the engine and the track? You own this train and its cargo, its route.

This is your life to imagine. Do not neglect the details.

Do not turn away from the quiet voices within; they speak of love, of destiny, of goodness. Do not silence the thoughts that tell you to slow down; they want to capture your attention and show you something grand. Do not ignore the heart that desires to rejoice; listen to the voices of the children at play, they delight. Learn to be delighted. Listen to the early-morning hum of your home, the quiet sounds before others awake.

Notice that what you see all around is beauty, no matter where you are, no matter what your state—right before your eyes beauty awaits.

Because yours is the breath, the glance, the one simple precious thought.

בָּרוּךְ אַתָּה, יְיָ אֱלֹהֵינוּ, מֶלֶךְ הָעוֹלָם, אֲשֶׁר קִדְּשָׁנוּ בְּמִצְוֹתָיו וְצִוָּנוּ עַל סְפִירַת הָעֹמֶר.

Baruch atah, Adonai Eloheinu, Melech haolam, asher kid'shanu b'mitzvotav v'tzivanu al s'firat haomer.

Praised be You, Adonai our God, who rules the universe, instilling within us the holiness of mitzvot by commanding us to count the Omer.

Today is the thirty-fifth day—five weeks of the Omer.

IMAGINATION

Within me a well, deep, filled with cool abundant water.

God,
sweet muse of love and loveliness!
Turn my thoughts toward You
that my eyes may see
and my heart may know
and my mind may remember
that there is beauty in my dreams.

Beyond me, a vision, a clear yet winding way.

Invisible God, eternal God
God of holiness and wonder
awaken my spirit so that
I may envision
and behold
and make real
a universe of light.

In the palm of my hand, all things possible.

Week Six:

Courage

And Moses, afraid, pleaded, *Please, O my God,*
I have never been a man of words . . .
I am slow of speech and slow of tongue.

And God simply said to him,
Who gives humans speech?
Who makes him dumb or deaf, seeing or blind?
Is it not I, the Eternal?

Exodus 4:11

Alone with his God, close to the fire of revelation, Moses reveals his deepest fear. So honest, such intimacy. The freedom of a nation, the destiny of a people depends on Moses's ability to persuade. And yet he cannot speak, eloquent expression eludes him. A simple confession to God—what I need most, he says, I do not have.

And God's answer? I know who you are. It is I, God, the creator of all things, who formed you. Do not despair of your imperfections. Strive to rise above limitations and attain all that is possible.

Such is the ironic fact of human nature: we protect our deficiencies and hide our inadequacies. But perhaps it should be the opposite. Perhaps we should protect our gifts, cherishing the good within us, and reveal our doubts, asking for help and support. That would take courage.

Tend to your soul with kindness. Accept your limitations with compassion. It takes courage to be the person you were always meant to be.

Decide to live another way. Discern the path before you. Choose to step onto the path. Live with hope in your heart. Imagine a vision of yourself living a life of splendor, of meaning, of purpose. Do not fear. Have courage.

36th Day of the Omer

There were no formerly heroic times, and there was no formerly pure generation. There is no one here but us chickens, and so it has always been: a people busy and powerful, knowledgeable, ambivalent, important, fearful, and self-aware; a people who scheme, promote, deceive, and conquer; who pray for their loved ones, and long to flee misery and skip death. . . .

There is no less holiness at this time. . . . In any instant the sacred may wipe you with its finger. In any instant the bush may flare, your feet may rise, or you may see a bunch of souls in the tree. In any instant you may avail yourself of the power to love your enemies; to accept failure, slander, or the grief of loss; or to endure torture.

Purity's time is always now. Purity is no social phenomenon, a cultural thing whose time we have missed. . . . "Each and every day the Divine Voice issues from Sinai," says the Talmud.

Annie Dillard, *For the Time Being*

The time is upon us, he said. The time for truth, and not anger. When you are angry, you are blinded to what is really true. You cannot see the light out of the maze of confusion and darkness. Anger blinds you. The time is upon us, he said. The time for courage, not cowardice. Courage requires that you simply do what you can. No more. But also no less. The time is upon us to reconcile. It does not matter who is right and who is wrong. All I really want is peace. Peace for myself and peace for my family.

בָּרוּךְ אַתָּה, יְיָ אֱלֹהֵינוּ, מֶלֶךְ הָעוֹלָם, אֲשֶׁר קִדְּשָׁנוּ בְּמִצְוֹתָיו וְצִוָּנוּ עַל סְפִירַת הָעֹמֶר.

Baruch atah, Adonai Eloheinu, Melech haolam, asher kid'shanu b'mitzvotav v'tzivanu al s'firat haomer.

Praised be You, Adonai our God, who rules the universe, instilling within us the holiness of mitzvot by commanding us to count the Omer.

Today is the thirty-sixth day—five weeks and one day of the Omer.

Though I have fallen, I rise again;
Though I sit in darkness, God is my light.

Micah 7:8

22 IYAR

37th Day of the Omer

Man is afraid of things that cannot harm him, and he knows it; and he craves things that cannot help him, and he knows it. But actually, it is something within man he is afraid of, and something within man that he craves. . .

When senseless hatred reigns on earth, and men hide their faces from one another, then heaven is forced to hide its face. But when love comes to rule the earth, and men reveal their faces to one another, then the splendor of God will be revealed.

Martin Buber, Ten Rungs: Collected Hasidic Sayings

Every now and then we have to drill a hole in the bottom of the boat that keeps us afloat. Because one simply should not chart a course carried by routine and complacency.

And though the tumble and rumble of fundamental change is chaotic and alarming and hard and disruptive and so frightening, and though it goes against our natural instinct to protect and defend who we are and what we know at all costs, sometimes the cost of staying the same is simply too great. Isn't it? To live in the routine of it all, bored, un-actualized is really hard. Right?

The courage you will need to drill the hole and the struggle you will experience to stay afloat will empower you, transform you, and enliven you. It will be like a birth. Out of the waters, a stronger more vitalized person.

Excellence, creative energy, passion, and a sense of purpose require something different. Remember: spiritual and intellectual growth sometimes is a journey of risk and courage.

Sometimes you have to drill a hole in the boat that keeps you afloat.

בָּרוּךְ אַתָּה, יְיָ אֱלֹהֵינוּ, מֶלֶךְ הָעוֹלָם, אֲשֶׁר קִדְּשָׁנוּ בְּמִצְוֹתָיו וְצִוָּנוּ עַל סְפִירַת הָעֹמֶר.

Baruch atah, Adonai Eloheinu, Melech haolam, asher kid'shanu b'mitzvotav v'tzivanu al s'firat haomer.

Praised be You, Adonai our God, who rules the universe, instilling within us the holiness of mitzvot by commanding us to count the Omer.

Today is the thirty-seventh day—five weeks and two days of the Omer.

23   IYAR

38th Day of the Omer

We have to trust that, when the time comes, God, who helps us know how to live, will help us know how to die. We must hope that God, who privileges us with the capacity to know justice, share love, and experience beauty, will also grant us generosity, humility, and wisdom, so that we can both live and let go of life well.

Jonathan Wittenberg, *The Eternal Journey:*
Meditations on the Jewish Year

Pursue the life that you wish to live. Be impatient with mediocrity. Do not abide sustained boredom. Care. Tell the children that they are created in the image of God. Tell them often. Be still enough to listen to your heart. Read. Practice obedience cautiously. Stand for something. Create. Make the following declaration: I will search for God. I will not betray my life's calling.

בָּרוּךְ אַתָּה, יְיָ אֱלֹהֵינוּ, מֶלֶךְ הָעוֹלָם, אֲשֶׁר קִדְּשָׁנוּ
בְּמִצְוֹתָיו וְצִוָּנוּ עַל סְפִירַת הָעְמֶר.

Baruch atah, Adonai Eloheinu, Melech haolam, asher kid'shanu
b'mitzvotav v'tzivanu al s'firat haomer.

Praised be You, Adonai our God, who rules the universe,
instilling within us the holiness of mitzvot by commanding us
to count the Omer.

Today is the thirty-eighth day—five weeks and three days of
the Omer.

24   IYAR

39th Day of the Omer

A foolish consistency is the hobgoblin of little minds, adored by little statesmen and philosophers and divines. With consistency a great soul has simply nothing to do. He may as well concern himself with his shadow on the wall. Speak what you think now in hard words and to-morrow speak what to-morrow thinks in hard words again, though it contradict every thing you said to-day.—"Ah, so you shall be sure to be misunderstood."—Is it so bad then to be misunderstood? . . . To be great is to be misunderstood.

Ralph Waldo Emerson, Self-Reliance

We chart a course for ourselves, and we walk along a road to meet our goals, to realize our ambitions. And though the course is well-considered, periodically we reach a barrier, as if suddenly someone has put up a brick wall that prevents us from moving forward. And we cannot proceed. So we have a choice: we can beat our head against the wall; we can sit there, and stare at the wall in dismay; we can try to climb over it, go around it, or dig under it; or, we can simply turn our head sharply to the left and see that there is another way, a different path.

Sometimes I think that obstacles and barriers are God's way of telling us to turn left. That is how our destiny unfolds. We stay the course, and then we make a turn, change direction, and then stay the course again. We are never really stuck, unless we choose to be. Stuck is a perspective. Barriers are invitations, obstacles, road signs.

בָּרוּךְ אַתָּה, יְיָ אֱלֹהֵינוּ, מֶלֶךְ הָעוֹלָם, אֲשֶׁר קִדְּשָׁנוּ
בְּמִצְוֹתָיו וְצִוָּנוּ עַל סְפִירַת הָעֹמֶר.

Baruch atah, Adonai Eloheinu, Melech haolam, asher kid'shanu b'mitzvotav v'tzivanu al s'firat haomer.

Praised be You, Adonai our God, who rules the universe, instilling within us the holiness of mitzvot by commanding us to count the Omer.

Today is the thirty-ninth day—five weeks and four days of the Omer.

A learned one of David;
a prayer when he was in a cave.
I cry to God with my voice,
With my cry I pray to You. . . .
Bring my soul out of prison,
that I may give thanks unto Your name.

PSALM 142:1–2, 8

25   IYAR

40th Day of the Omer

The first thing that Isaac learned was that his mother, Sarah, had died....
On their journey up to the mountain, Abraham had told Isaac that every-
thing would be all right. No one would ever be able to tell him that again.
The rabbis refer to Isaac's God as *Pachad Yitzchak*, the Fear of Isaac.

After the traumatic encounter on the mountain, the rabbis ask, "And
Isaac, where was he?" They answer, "The Holy One brought him into the
Garden of Eden and there he stayed three years." What was he doing all
that time in Paradise? The midrash tells us, "The angels were healing him."

So many times when we confront difficulties, when we are hurt or
face loss, people tell us we will get over it, everything will be okay. But
I don't imagine Isaac ever got over it; rather, the angels taught him how
to heal, how to get on with it.

The name of Isaac's God means "fear," but Isaac's name means "laughter." . . . The angels taught him to laugh in the face of the unknown and
wrestle joy out of despair. . . . I believe the angels taught him to forget some
things and forgive others. We easily forget appointments, but we remember
grudges for years. We misplace things but never resentments. . . . Whenever
confronted with my personal trials and fears, I try to heed the wisdom of
Isaac's healing angels. Find support in one another. Forget some things and
forgive others. Laugh whenever possible and celebrate whenever you can.
Embrace the present moment. And never, never give up hope.

Rabbi Sandy Eisenberg Sasso,
Midrash, Reading the Bible with Question Marks

What we think we know about the future, we make up. We make assumptions so that we can plan and justify our way of living. We think we understand what is true and right, what is important and necessary, what is a priority and what is essential.

And that is OK. Until it's not.

And then something happens: a diagnosis, a shift in relationships, a tremor at work, a death . . . and the valley casts a shadow and we walk in a fog, dazed, finally understanding how oblivious we have been to what is really important. So we refocus our lives and something odd happens. The colors are brighter, and the laughter is poignant, and the silliness is truly silly, and slowing down does not seem like a waste of time, and friendships are redefined, and our words have meaning.

Because in the valley of shadows, there is clarity. Do not fear.

בָּרוּךְ אַתָּה, יְיָ אֱלֹהֵינוּ, מֶלֶךְ הָעוֹלָם, אֲשֶׁר קִדְּשָׁנוּ בְּמִצְוֹתָיו וְצִוָּנוּ עַל סְפִירַת הָעֹמֶר.

Baruch atah, Adonai Eloheinu, Melech haolam, asher kid'shanu b'mitzvotav v'tzivanu al s'firat haomer.

Praised be You, Adonai our God, who rules the universe, instilling within us the holiness of mitzvot by commanding us to count the Omer.

Today is the fortieth day—five weeks and five days of the Omer.

26 IYAR

41st Day of the Omer

I am a bow in your hand, Lord. Draw me, lest I rot.

Do not overdraw me, Lord. I shall break.

Overdraw me, Lord, and who cares if I break!

Nikos Kazantzakis, Report to Greco

To be in service to something larger than ourselves is true greatness. It is the work of our lives.

Let there be no confusion: you may not be earning a living by doing your work. Your work is your contract with God. It requires you to use unique abilities, your natural inclination, and your passion. Your work is your purpose for living; it is service to great and noble things. We all have met the English teacher who tends to wounded souls, the doctor who motivates sacred living, the administrative assistant who teaches joy, the corporate VP who inspires greatness. Beyond the resume, the paycheck, the job description, there is work to be done. Past the reviews and the advancements, and the office politics, there is a world to embrace.

Do not confuse your job with your work. I learned a while ago that the best way to play politics is not to play. You may lose your job, but you will not lose your integrity. Stay true to your Work. It is your true legacy.

בָּרוּךְ אַתָּה, יְיָ אֱלֹהֵינוּ, מֶלֶךְ הָעוֹלָם, אֲשֶׁר קִדְּשָׁנוּ
בְּמִצְוֹתָיו וְצִוָּנוּ עַל סְפִירַת הָעֹמֶר.

Baruch atah, Adonai Eloheinu, Melech haolam, asher kid'shanu
b'mitzvotav v'tzivanu al s'firat haomer.

Praised be You, Adonai our God, who rules the universe,
instilling within us the holiness of mitzvot by commanding us
to count the Omer.

Today is the forty-first day—five weeks and six days of the Omer.

27   IYAR

42nd Day of the Omer

Just as the winged energy of delight
carried you over many chasms early on,
now raise the daringly imagined arch
holding up the astounding bridges.

Miracle doesn't lie only in the amazing
living through and defeat of danger;
miracles become miracles in the clear
achievement that is earned.

To work with things is not hubris
when building the association beyond words;
denser and denser the pattern becomes—
being carried along is not enough.

Take your well-disciplined strengths
And stretch them between two
opposing poles. Because inside human beings
is where God learns.

Rainer Maria Rilke, in *Selected Poems of Rainer Maria Rilke,*
edited and translated by Robert Bly

All my life I have fought for three things: the freedom to think creatively, the trust to love completely, the courage to heal what is broken. All I can say is that after so many years, I am still so very far from myself.

Find the way to live beyond the boundaries. Because within the well-tended fence of our soul we hold on to so much that we no longer need. We cling to the weight of our lives, thinking that it saves us, grounds us, keeps us from drifting too far from our past. But drift we must, if what holds us keeps us down.

This is what I mean to say: with all the strength and might that you have, dare to live, to be whole again, not fragmented by memory and pain.

And then approach with humility the Holy One, that invisible, mysterious, unity that is the source of light. Creative spirit. Spirit of goodness and aspiration. Source of love.

בָּרוּךְ אַתָּה, יְיָ אֱלֹהֵינוּ, מֶלֶךְ הָעוֹלָם, אֲשֶׁר קִדְּשָׁנוּ
בְּמִצְוֹתָיו וְצִוָּנוּ עַל סְפִירַת הָעֹמֶר.

Baruch atah, Adonai Eloheinu, Melech haolam, asher kid'shanu
b'mitzvotav v'tzivanu al s'firat haomer.

Praised be You, Adonai our God, who rules the universe,
instilling within us the holiness of mitzvot by commanding us
to count the Omer.

Today is the forty-second day—six weeks of the Omer.

COURAGE

And I said:
O if only I had wings like the dove
I would fly away and find a restful abode.
I would wander afar while hastening
to find a haven from the stormy tempest. (PSALM 55:7–9)

And so I pray
that my spirit have the strength to soar,
that my heart have the courage to seek,
and my mind the wisdom to discover,
a life of meaning and purpose.

Grant me, O God,
strength,
courage,
and wisdom.

Week Seven:

Pray

Moses and Aaron said to Pharaoh,

Thus says the Eternal, the God of Israel:

Let My people go that they may celebrate

a festival for Me in the wilderness.

Exodus 5:1

This is the great journey: To refine our lives. To become strong and resolved, to have meaning and purpose, depth and commitment. To live in awe and wonder and to bear witness to life's grandeur.

Have an active conversation with the invisible: doubt and argue, dream and beg, ask for help, ask for forgiveness, offer gratitude. Shout at the heavens when you despair, and raise your voice in song when you rejoice. Sit still through the silences of the spirit; do not run from what cannot be known or understood. Life is mystery. Anything we truly want to know and understand is, by definition, mysterious.

Decide. Choose. Discern. Hope. Imagine. Have courage.

Pray. When we pray, we bow in humility to the Greatness of it all.

May our lives become a prayer to all that is good and important.

And know: life is given meaning, texture, purpose when, meekly, we utter amen to the mystery and magnificence of life.

43rd Day of the Omer

Learn to be quiet.
You need not do anything.

Remain sitting at your table and listen.

You need not even listen, just wait.

You need not even wait,
just learn to be quiet, still and solitary.

And the world will freely offer itself to you unmasked.

It has no choice,
it will roll in ecstasy at your feet.

Franz Kafka

The window in my study is alive; the entire east wall reveals without comment and without judgment the trees upon the lane. For weeks now I have been watching the silent transformation from bare branch, to small wisps of green, to lush canopies of leaves that move in the wind, flicker in the light, quiver in the rain.

A silent spectacle.

And beyond the trees, the sun rises quiet as the breath of God.
And beyond the sun, sky, sometimes pale, sometimes blue, sometimes
magenta, sometimes still, sometimes in motion, depends on the day.

Also silent.

And in my study, in the corner, turned toward the window and the
lane with its trees and rising sun and sky, I often sit, a student, a child
really, trying to learn what it all means.

בָּרוּךְ אַתָּה, יְיָ אֱלֹהֵינוּ, מֶלֶךְ הָעוֹלָם, אֲשֶׁר קִדְּשָׁנוּ
בְּמִצְוֹתָיו וְצִוָּנוּ עַל סְפִירַת הָעֹמֶר.

Baruch atah, Adonai Eloheinu, Melech haolam, asher kid'shanu
b'mitzvotav v'tzivanu al s'firat haomer.

Praised be You, Adonai our God, who rules the universe,
instilling within us the holiness of mitzvot by commanding us
to count the Omer.

Today is the forty-third day—six weeks and one day of the Omer.

29   IYAR

44th Day of the Omer

[The] creative God is the One who made us co-creators of this created universe. We cooperate in the seeding of life. We participate in the coming of justice. We cultivate the ground. God created the world, yes, but then gave it to us to develop. We have made it what it is.

It is faith in this God that raises us up from our tombs of oppression and sadness and want and fear and pain to begin again doing our part to make the world a laughing, loving place.

There is no reason to assume, for example, that God will end nuclear weaponry. If the world ends in a nuclear blast, it will not be this God who did it. We created nuclear weapons; we can end them ourselves. . . . In the light of everything we have been given, we have no grounds for blaming God for our losses. . . .

The call to faith is not the call to surrender to a grinning, ghoulish God who tries creation for the sheer delight of trial. . . .

What are we called to believe and in whom? We are surely called to believe that God who is everywhere is with us. And we are called to believe that this God is Energy and Love. Not the Grand Inquisitor. Not the great Circus Master. Not the Indifferent Professor who does distant research on our lives. God is the One who made for us a good world and walks with us to hold us up as we go. Sometimes, in the face of the God of life, the most faithful thing we can do is simply to keep on living.

Joan D. Chittister, *Scarred by Struggle, Transformed by Hope*

Sometimes my response to prayer is a simple "no" (though "no" is never truly simple). Sometimes it is a foot-tapping impatience or a stubborn resistance. Then there are times when I pray and the most honest response I can muster is an angry fist shaking wildly at the heavens. And sometimes my response to prayer is an audible, discernible, from the gut "sigh."

And then, sometimes the spirit of God is upon me, and there is silence all around, and I feel the vibrations of other people's supplications in my very being. During those precious moments, my response is to their prayer, and it is a simple nod, and a shrug of the shoulders at the mystery of life.

בָּרוּךְ אַתָּה, יְיָ אֱלֹהֵינוּ, מֶלֶךְ הָעוֹלָם, אֲשֶׁר קִדְּשָׁנוּ
בְּמִצְוֹתָיו וְצִוָּנוּ עַל סְפִירַת הָעֹמֶר.

Baruch atah, Adonai Eloheinu, Melech haolam, asher ḳid'shanu b'mitzvotav v'tzivanu al s'firat haomer.

Praised be You, Adonai our God, who rules the universe, instilling within us the holiness of mitzvot by commanding us to count the Omer.

Today is the forty-fourth day—six weeks and two days of the Omer.

1   SIVAN

45th Day of the Omer

Bird tracks in the sand on the seashore
like the handwriting of someone who jotted down
words, names, numbers and places, so he would remember.
Bird tracks in the sand at night
are still there in the daytime, though I've never seen
the bird that left them. That's the way it is
with God.

"Gods Change, Prayers Are Here to Stay"
in Yehuda Amichai, *Open Closed Open: Poems,*
translated by Chana Bloch and Chana Kronfeld

If it's nature then go—go to the surprise that awaits daily—each wave brings a message, every tree sings of majesty, the flowers, the harsh changes of weather, the mountain, the sea. It doesn't matter except that you go to be a part of it all.

And if it's people, then engage—each meeting filled with the chatter of voices, the simplicity of touch, the compassion, the curiosity, the fierce intelligence, the unpredictable behaviors.

And if it is the sanctuary, then join—a community of strangers, of friends, of acquaintances, singing in unison, wondering in unison, praying in unison, silent in unison.

This is what is meant by God is everywhere. God in the elements, in the encounter, in the community, in the silence, in the creativity, in the gut, in the meadow, in the eyes of the beholder, in the heart of the beholden, in the question, in the anguish, in the joy.

Go and meet your God.

בָּרוּךְ אַתָּה, יְיָ אֱלֹהֵינוּ, מֶלֶךְ הָעוֹלָם, אֲשֶׁר קִדְּשָׁנוּ בְּמִצְוֹתָיו וְצִוָּנוּ עַל סְפִירַת הָעֹמֶר.

Baruch atah, Adonai Eloheinu, Melech haolam, asher kid'shanu b'mitzvotav v'tzivanu al s'firat haomer.

Praised be You, Adonai our God, who rules the universe, instilling within us the holiness of mitzvot by commanding us to count the Omer.

Today is the forty-fifth day—six weeks and three days of the Omer.

Sing a new song unto God.

Sing to God, all the earth. . . .

Proclaim God's victory day after day.

Psalm 96:1–2

2 SIVAN

46th Day of the Omer

I live in a lovely suburban neighborhood, but quite near a freeway off-ramp. Cars come careening onto Densmore Avenue at a high rate of speed, rushing onto the main thoroughfare of Ventura Boulevard. Our synagogue, Valley Beth Shalom, is four blocks from our home. A day school, a preschool, and an afternoon religious school are on its campus; children walk across Densmore all day long to reach the congregation's parking lot. It is a potentially dangerous situation. Signs are posted: "School Zone," "Danger: Children Crossing." But, mostly, the signs are ignored.

Then, one day, two huge trucks arrived on our street and began to install speed bumps—small hills of asphalt designed to slow down speeding cars. In the middle of each of the four blocks, another speed bump was built. And, lo and behold, cars began to slow down . . . and the neighborhood felt safer, slower. Since I travel the street almost every day, I fear what the bumps are doing to my shock absorbers, but I figure it's worth it if the children are out of harm's way.

This is the reason for reciting one hundred blessings every day: to slow us down so we can appreciate what surrounds us. . . .

Each blessing is a rendezvous with God, a way to heighten a personal relationship with heaven as we enjoy the evidence of God's presence on earth.

Dr. Ron Wolfson, *The Seven Questions You're Asked in Heaven: Reviewing and Renewing Your Life on Earth*

Once, before a half-filled grave, I stood next to the grandson of the man we were burying. Everyone had gone back to their cars, but he would not leave. The boy must have been near bar mitzvah age. He was softly crying. I whispered words of comfort to him, to lessen the fear, to ease the grief. I told him that we cannot bury the spirit, only the body. That the good and sacred that was his grandfather was like a light that will always shine.

He was still weeping and then he said something that was barely audible. He said that he had wiped his tears with a tissue, threw the tissue into the grave and then covered it with earth, so that Papa would know they were all very sad. I put my arm around his shoulder and told him that, at that moment, his Papa was pure love and would be very proud of him.

This is what is meant by the invisible light. It is the light of the sacred, the tears of a child, and a simple act of love, intertwined in an unexpected moment. It is a prayer so gentle and sincere that all that is left for us to say is "amen."

בָּרוּךְ אַתָּה, יְיָ אֱלֹהֵינוּ, מֶלֶךְ הָעוֹלָם, אֲשֶׁר קִדְּשָׁנוּ בְּמִצְוֹתָיו וְצִוָּנוּ עַל סְפִירַת הָעֹמֶר.

Baruch atah, Adonai Eloheinu, Melech haolam, asher kid'shanu b'mitzvotav v'tzivanu al s'firat haomer.

Praised be You, Adonai our God, who rules the universe, instilling within us the holiness of mitzvot by commanding us to count the Omer.

Today is the forty-sixth day—six weeks and four days of the Omer.

47th Day of the Omer

God: I am that which is not.
Search and you shall find
about your universe of thought
only My shadow; grasp
only to hold the measure of your grip.
So am I God—therefore let go!

Jacob: I will not let you go.

"The Struggle" by Amy K. Blank, in *The Struggle and Other Poems*

Remember when your children were young and you gave them something that they wanted, like a cookie, and then said, "Now what do you say?" How many times did you go through that routine? How many years until they learned to say thank you?

It seems that gratitude is a practice.

The most powerful prayer is not "please" or "why" or even "may I," but rather "thank you." Imagine how your life would be different if upon waking every morning you uttered a prayer of gratitude. Imagine how your life would be different if every day you said, "Thank You, God, for Your abundant gifts," even when life is difficult. How would that shift your perspective, change your outlook on life?

We affirm the goodness in life when we offer a daily prayer of gratitude. When life is difficult, and still we find the spiritual fortitude to offer a prayer of gratitude, then we declare possibility, optimism, hope.

Gratitude and hope are the spiritual foundations of a life of meaning and purpose.

בָּרוּךְ אַתָּה, יְיָ אֱלֹהֵינוּ, מֶלֶךְ הָעוֹלָם, אֲשֶׁר קִדְּשָׁנוּ בְּמִצְוֹתָיו וְצִוָּנוּ עַל סְפִירַת הָעֹמֶר.

Baruch atah, Adonai Eloheinu, Melech haolam, asher kid'shanu b'mitzvotav v'tzivanu al s'firat haomer.

Praised be You, Adonai our God, who rules the universe, instilling within us the holiness of mitzvot by commanding us to count the Omer.

Today is the forty-seventh day—six weeks and five days of the Omer.

4 SIVAN

48th Day of the Omer

At the center of our worship stands a cry. The cry itself is beyond worship, almost beyond words. All of our prayers, the ordered literary creation of our best rabbinic minds, serve as mere accompaniment to this cry. They prepare us for it, lead us up to the appropriate moment, coax the cry forth from deep within us, and then gently guide us back from it.

The cry itself—Sh'ma Yisra'el—"Hear O Israel, Y-H-W-H our God, Y-H-W-H is One!"—is not addressed to God. It is a call to Israel, to ourselves and those around us. It is a call to all who struggle with the divine and the human, who struggle to understand. It is our cry to one another; we call it out as the angels call out, "Holy, holy, holy!" This act of calling demands all our strength; sometimes it even demands life itself.

Rabbi Arthur Green, *Seek My Face: A Jewish Mystical Theology*

Some say the glass is half empty. Some say the glass is half full. I say our cup runneth over (Psalm 23:5). This is the meaning of the verse "Surely goodness and mercy shall follow you all the days of your life" (Psalm 23:6). Allow your life to overflow with goodness and mercy.

It was once said of a woman in her eulogy that she made the cup twice the size it had to be. That, too. That, too.

בָּרוּךְ אַתָּה, יְיָ אֱלֹהֵינוּ, מֶלֶךְ הָעוֹלָם, אֲשֶׁר קִדְּשָׁנוּ
בְּמִצְוֹתָיו וְצִוָּנוּ עַל סְפִירַת הָעֹמֶר.

*Baruch atah, Adonai Eloheinu, Melech haolam, asher kid'shanu
b'mitzvotav v'tzivanu al s'firat haomer.*

Praised be You, Adonai our God, who rules the universe,
instilling within us the holiness of mitzvot by commanding us
to count the Omer.

Today is the forty-eighth day—six weeks and six days of the Omer.

By day God is kindness,
by night God's song is with me.

PSALM 42:9

5 SIVAN

49th and last day of the Omer

I prayed for wonders instead of happiness,
and You gave them to me.

Rabbi Abraham Joshua Heschel,
The Ineffable Name of God: Man; Poems

Never forget that as you proceed upon the path, you leave behind traces in the hearts of those you have loved and those you have denied; you leave impressions in the memories of those you have hurt and those you have encouraged; you touch the spirits of those you have embraced and those you have shunned.

It is a great responsibility to live.

And know, of all the words I have found, kindness is the most powerful. It can transform the world. At the end of my days, the only thing I will regret in my life are times when I was unkind.

בָּרוּךְ אַתָּה, יְיָ אֱלֹהֵינוּ, מֶלֶךְ הָעוֹלָם, אֲשֶׁר קִדְּשָׁנוּ
בְּמִצְוֹתָיו וְצִוָּנוּ עַל סְפִירַת הָעֹמֶר.

Baruch atah, Adonai Eloheinu, Melech haolam, asher kid'shanu b'mitzvotav v'tzivanu al s'firat haomer.

Praised be You, Adonai our God, who rules the universe, instilling within us the holiness of mitzvot by commanding us to count the Omer.

Today is the forty-ninth day—seven weeks of the Omer.

PRAYER

May I see the spark of holiness in all that I do.
May the light of God guide me through darkness.

May my prayers strengthen me,
urging me to be present for those who are suffering.

May I become a messenger of caring and compassion,
a partner with God in the work of healing.

May I be guided to fight injustice
and to love peace and harmony.

May God's blessing be with those who are in my heart,
as I utter this prayer.

May all that is good in life lead me to passion and radiance.
By Your light, O God, may I see light.

COUNTING'S END

I have numbered my days and come to understand that my days are numbered. The finite nature of my life demands my attention and constant consideration. I have been granted daily life in order to think, to contemplate, to be kind, to be purposeful, to be silent, to be energetic, to be god-like, to be fully human, to be forgiving, to be in love, to be aware of life with all aspects of my being, with my mind, my body, my spirit.

I have numbered my days and have come to understand that each day is an invitation:

- Today: an invitation to become present
- The day before: an invitation to be reflective
- The day after: an invitation to become repentant
- Not today: an invitation to be discerning
- Tomorrow: an invitation to anticipate
- Yesterday: an invitation to remember
- Never again: an invitation to commit
- Someday: an invitation to dream
- Most days: an invitation to cultivate discipline
- Until the day of all days, the last day: an invitation into eternity

For
Special
Days

YOM HASHOAH:
HOLOCAUST REMEMBRANCE DAY

The Lord is my shepherd,
    I will not bleat.
    But I shall want,
    because the world is want—
    is stones instead of pasture.
    I will be stubborn, stand into the wind.

He restoreth my soul . . .
    But should he not replenish
    I will dredge up clarity,
    and ask no fanciful reward.
    To hold my brother's hand
    shall be my righteousness.

In the valley of deep darkness
    his rod will goad me on,
    his staff not mine to lean upon.

In the presence of my enemies
    I am afraid.
    Oh! Let me not deceive myself;

it is not said who
shall sit down and eat.

And yet . . . and yet . . .

My cup runneth over
with vintage of the ripened vine.
There is, despite,
a spring of birds in me.

Goodness and mercy
and hope before the sun
follow into the night.

And I shall dwell
whether by quiet waters
or on shifting sands—
still in his house.

"Eisegesis" by Amy K. Blank, in *"I Know Four" and Other Things*

YOM HAZIKARON:
ISRAEL MEMORIAL DAY

But man does not live forever, and he should put the days of his life to the best possible use. He should try to live life to its fullest. How to do this I can't tell you. If I had a clear answer, I'd have half the solution to the puzzle called life. I only know that I don't want to reach a certain age, look around me and suddenly discover that I've created nothing, that I'm like all the other human beings who dash about like so many insects, back and forth, never accomplishing anything, endlessly repeating the routine of their existence only to descend to their graves, leaving behind them progeny that will merely repeat the same "nothingness." (May 23, 1963)

In another week I'll be twenty-three. Time flies, doesn't it? My years bear down on me with all their weight. Not as a load or a burden, but as the sum of all the long and short moments that have gone into them. On me, on us, the young men of Israel, rests the duty of keeping our country safe. This is a heavy responsibility, which matures us early. It seems that the young Israeli belongs to a special breed of men. It's hard to explain this, but it can be felt. . . . In another week I'll be twenty-three, and I do not regret what I have done and what I'm about to do. I'm convinced that what I am doing is right. I believe in myself, in my country and in my future. I also believe in my family. That's a great deal for a man of my age who has already managed to feel very young and very old. (March 17, 1969)

The Letters of Jonathan Netanyahu: The Commander of the Entebbe Rescue Force

YOM HAATZMAUT:
ISRAEL INDEPENDENCE DAY

Once I was sitting on the steps near the gate at David's Citadel and I put down my two heavy baskets beside me. A group of tourists stood there around their guide, and I became their point of reference. "You see that man over there with the baskets? A little to the right of his head there's an arch from the Roman period. A little to the right of his head." "But he's moving, he's moving!" I said to myself: Redemption will come only when they are told, "Do you see that arch over there from the Roman period? It doesn't matter, but near it, a little to the left and then down a bit, there's a man who has just bought fruit and vegetables for his family."

"Tourists" by Yehuda Amichai,
in *The Selected Poetry of Yehuda Amichai*,
translated by Chana Bloch and Stephen Mitchell

EARTH DAY

Rabbi Shimon bar Yochai said:
Three things are of equal importance—
earth, humans, and rain.
Rabbi Levi ben Chiyata said:
. . . To teach that without earth, there is no rain,
and without rain, the earth cannot endure,
and without either,
humans cannot exist. (*B'reishit Rabbah* 13:3)
Rabbi Yochanan ben Zakkai . . . used to say:
If you have a sapling in your hand,
and someone should say to you that
the Messiah has come,
stay and complete the planting, and then go
to greet the Messiah. (*Avot D'Rabbi Natan* 31b)
When you reap the harvest of your land,
you shall not reap all the way
to the edges of your field, or gather
the gleanings of your harvest . . .
but you shall leave them
for the poor and the stranger:
I the Eternal am your God. (Leviticus 19:9–10)
But ask the beasts, and they will teach you;
the birds of the sky, and they will tell you;

or speak to the earth and it will teach you;

the fish of the sea, they will inform you.

Who among all these does not know

that the hand of the Eternal has done this? (Job 12:7–9)

Compiled by Rabbi Karyn D. Kedar

MOTHER'S DAY

Children, heed the discipline of a father;
Listen and learn discernment,
For I give you a good doctrine,
Forsake not my Torah.

Once I was a child to my father,
Tender and special to my mother.
I learned and they said to me,
Let your heart hold fast to my words,
Keep my commandments, live by them.
Acquire wisdom, acquire discernment;
Do not forget,
Do not stray from my teachings.
Do not forsake her and she will guard you;
Love her and she will protect you.
Begin with Wisdom, acquire wisdom;
With all your means acquire discernment.
Hold her and she will exalt you;
Embrace her,
She will bring you honor.

Proverbs 4:1–8

MEMORIAL DAY

I, may I rest in peace—I, who am still living, say,
May I have peace in the rest of my life.
I want peace right now while I'm still alive.
I don't want to wait like that pious man who wished for one leg
of the golden chair of Paradise, I want a four-legged chair
right here, a plain wooden chair. I want the rest of my peace now.
I have lived out my life in wars of every kind: battles without
and within, close combat, face-to-face, the faces always
my own, my lover-face, my enemy-face.
Wars with the old weapons—sticks and stones, blunt axe, words,
dull ripping knife, love and hate,
and wars with newfangled weapons—machine gun, missile,
words, land mines exploding, love and hate.
I don't want to fulfill my parents' prophecy that life is war.
I want peace with all my body and all my soul.
Rest me in peace.

"In My Life, On My Life"
by Yehuda Amichai, in *Open Closed Open: Poems,*
translated by Chana Bloch and Chana Kronfeld

SHABBAT 1

It's so stupid.
Wednesday afternoon,
soaked in the idiotica of errands
and all those "things to do"
that steal a man's minutes, his years—
I forgot the Queen.
Her Majesty was due at four-eighteen
on Friday, not a minute later,
and I was wasting hands, words, steps,
racing to a rushing finish-line
of roaring insignificance
I just as well could fill
with preparations for the royal entourage:
cleaning and cleansing each act's doing,
each word's saying,
in anticipation of the Great Event of Shabbas.

Who am I that she should wish
to spend the day with me?
I dry out my strengths, cook, move dust,
casually insensitive to all the songs
reminding me that she, the Queen,
in diamond-ruby-emerald-glow tiara,

would come to grace my table.
She comes,
no matter how the week was spent,
in joy or in silliness,
yet she comes.
And I am her host,
laying a linen flower tablecloth
that is white,
that is all the colors of the rainbow.

This is the Jews' sense of royalty:
she never does not spend one day a week
with me, and every Jew,
in the open air of freedom,
or lightening the misery of prisoners
in stinking Russian prisons
or the ghettoes of Damascus.

Come, my Shabbas Queen,
embodiment of Worlds-to-Be:
Your gracious kindness is our breath of life,
and though we once, twice, all-too-often
fail to say, "How beautiful your cape!
How lovely your hair, your Shechina-eyes!"
we will not always be so lax,
apathetic to your grace, your presence.
Touch us again this week
with your most unique love's tenderness,
and we shall sing to you our songs,

dance our dances in your honor,
and sigh for you our sighs
of longing, peace, and hope.

"Erev Shabbas" by Danny Siegel, in *Nine Entered Paradise Alive*

SHABBAT 2

I quarreled with kings till the Sabbath,
I fought with the six kings
of the six days of the week.

Sunday they took away my sleep.
Monday they scattered my salt.
And on the third day, my God,
they threw out my bread: whips flashed
across my face. The fourth day
they caught my dove, my flying dove,
and slaughtered it.
It was like that till Friday morning.

This is my whole week,
the dove's flight dying.

At nightfall Friday
I lit four candles,
and the queen of the Sabbath came to me.
Her face lit up the whole world,
and made it all a Sabbath.
My scattered salt
shone in its little bowl,

and my dove, my flying dove,
clapped its wings together,
and licked its throat.
The Sabbath queen blessed my candles,
and they burned with a pure, clean flame.
The light put out the days of the week
and my quarreling with the six kings.

The greenness of the mountains
is the greenness of the Sabbath.
The silver of the lake
is the silver of the Sabbath.
The singing of the wind
is the singing of the Sabbath.

And my heart's song
is an eternal Sabbath.

"Song of the Sabbath" by Kadya Molodowsky,
translated by Jean Valentine, in *A Treasury of Yiddish Poetry*,
edited by Irving Howe and Eliezer Greenberg

SHABBAT 3

The humble person judges all people on the scales of merit. One of the tzaddikim [righteous] was once asked: "How did you merit becoming master of the men of your generation?" He answered: "By regarding every man I saw as better than I. If he were wiser than I, I said: 'He also fears God more than I do because of his great wisdom.' If he were not so wise as I, I said: 'His sins are unintentional and mine are willful.' If he were older than I, I said: 'His merits are more than mine.' If I were older than he, I said: 'His sins are fewer than mine.' If he were my equal in wisdom and years, I said: 'His heart is better to God than mine, for I know the sins that I have committed, but I do not know his.' If he were richer than I, I said: 'He gives more charity than I do.' If he were poorer, I said: 'He is of a more contrite and lowly spirit than I, and he is better than I.' So saying, I honored all men and humbled myself before them."

. . . They tell of a certain king who one night, when many men were sitting before him, got up and tended to the lamp himself so that it would not go out. When he was asked why he did not order another to take care of it, he replied: "I arose a king and returned a king."

Adapted from *The Ways of the Tzaddikim*,
edited by Rabbi Gavriel Zaloshinsky

SHABBAT 4

What more is there to say? The only "hidden treasures" we need seek out are those hidden by God Himself, and these are hidden throughout reality. The only houses we need to destroy in order to find them are those walls we ourselves construct, the blinders we keep setting up to keep us from seeing the light within. We are our own Canaanites; we are our only Israel.

Rabbi Arthur Green, The Language of Truth

SHABBAT 5

The perception that dawns on a person to see the world not as finished, but as in the process of continued becoming, ascending, developing—this changes him from being "under the sun" to being "above the sun," from the place where there is nothing new to the place where there is nothing old, where everything takes on new form. The joy of heaven and earth abides in him as on the day they were created.

In this luminous perspective one looks at all the worlds, at the general and the human development, at the destiny of each creature, at all the events of all times.

The time that is an uninterrupted Sabbath on which eternal peace shines, is the day when, by the nature of its creation, there pulsates a continued thrust for newness. It needs no end, no termination. It is the choicest of days, an ornament of beauty, the source of all blessings.

Rabbi Abraham Isaac Kook,
The Lights of Penitence, the Moral Principles,
Lights of Holiness, Essays, Letters, and Poems

SHABBAT 6

The seventh day sings. An old allegory asserts: "When Adam saw the majesty of the Sabbath, its greatness and glory, and the joy it conferred upon all beings, he intoned a song of praise for the Sabbath day as if *to give thanks to the Sabbath day.* Then God said to him: Thou singest a song of praise to the Sabbath day, and singest none to Me, the God of the Sabbath? Thereupon the Sabbath rose from its seat, and prostrated herself before God, saying: It is a good thing *to give thanks unto the Lord.* And the whole of creation added: And to sing praise unto Thy Name, O Most High."

"Angels have six wings, one for each day of the week, with which they chant their song; but they remain silent on the Sabbath, for it is the Sabbath which then chants a hymn to God." It is the Sabbath that inspires all the creatures to sing praise to the Lord.

Rabbi Abraham Joshua Heschel,
The Sabbath: Its Meaning for Modern Man

SHABBAT 7

Human beings have always dreamed of a utopia where all will be good. No such place exists. When people believe that religion makes them God's special favorites, they risk the hubris that diminishes their compassion for others. When they believe some other human system absolves them from the daily struggle to be good, because all that matters is the noble enterprise, they risk even greater evil. As that wise observer of the human condition, Alexis de Tocqueville, wrote: "As long as man has religion, he will not believe in his own perfectibility."

Rabbi David J. Wolpe, *Why Faith Matters*

SHABBAT 8

What shall you do?
Work yourself to distraction?
Distract yourself from work?
Neither extreme is desirable.
Better the middle way:
eat and enjoy your food in the company of friends;
work and enjoy the capacities of body and mind.
In this world of seeming separation and divided minds,
there is no escape from impermanence.
Do not build a fortress against loss
or lay siege to eternity.
Rather, open your eyes to the wonder of the fleeting
and make of each moment an opportunity to do what needs doing.

Your days are few and you cannot know which will be your last.
Appreciate the moment.
Sharpen your mind.
Live with attention.
Live without expectation.
And let sorrow and joy take care of themselves.

Ecclesiastes 5:17–19 as interpreted by Rabbi Rami Shapiro,
in *The Way of Solomon: Finding Joy and
Contentment in the Wisdom of Ecclesiastes*

LAG BAOMER

My God breathes by my side
let Him not stop breathing.
When all is blocked one hears in the quiet
the hidden distress of the rocks
and the sound of much dew pouring on them
ever since Moses hit them.

"My God Breathes by My Side,"
in *These Mountains: Selected Poems of Rivka Miriam,*
translated by Linda Zisquit

ROSH CHODESH

Most of us succumb to the majestic property of things and evaluate events by their tangible results. We appreciate things that are displayed in the realm of Space. The truth, however, is that the genuinely precious is encountered in the realm of Time, rather than in Spaces. Feelings, thoughts, are our own, while possessions are alien and often treacherous to the self. To be is more essential than to have. Though we deal with things, we live in deeds.

Rabbi Abraham Joshua Heschel, *The Earth is the Lord's:*
The Inner World of the Jew in Eastern Europe

Permissions

Every effort has been made to ascertain the owners of copyrights for the selections used in this volume and to obtain permission to reprint copyrighted passages. The Central Conference of American Rabbis expresses gratitude for permissions it has received. The Conference will be pleased, in subsequent editions, to correct any inadvertent errors or omissions that may be pointed out.

PERMISSIONS

186   The perception that dawns on a person, from *Abraham Isaac Kook, The Lights of Penitence, The Moral Principles, Lights of Holiness, Essays, Letters, and Poems*, edited by Ben Zion Bobsker © 1978 by Paulist Press, p. 229.

187   The seventh day sings, by Abraham Joshua Heschel, in *The Sabbath* © 1951 by Farrar, Straus and Giroux, pp. 23-24.

188   Human beings have always dreamed of a utopia, by David Wolpe, in *Why Faith Matters* © 2008 by HarperCollins Publishers, Inc., p. 78. Used by permission.

189   "What Shall You Do?" by Rami Shapiro, in *The Way of Solomon* © 2000 by HarperCollins Publishers, Inc., p. 51.

190   "My God Breathes by My Side," by Rivka Miriam, in *These Mountains: Selected Poems of Rivka Miriam* © 2009 by Toby Press. Used by permission.

191   Most of us succumb to the majestic property, by Abraham Joshua Heschel in *The Earth Is the Lord's: The Inner World of the Jew in Eastern Europe* © 1950 by Farrar, Straus and Giroux.

Rabbi Karyn D. Kedar is the senior rabbi at Congregation BJBE in the Chicago area. Her previously published books include *God Whispers, The Dance of the Dolphin (Our Dance with God)*, and *The Bridge to Forgiveness*. She is published in numerous anthologies and is renowned for her creative liturgy.

Rabbi Kedar teaches courses and leads retreats that explore the need for meaning and purpose in our busy lives, creating an intentional life, spiritual awakening, forgiveness, as well as inspirational leadership and creating the synagogue for the twenty-first century. She believes that vision and imagination, the persistent pursuit of light, and the practice of kindness reveal the path to a meaningful and purposeful life.

She and her husband Ezra are the proud parents of Talia, Moti, Shiri, and Ilan and grandparents of Lihi and Maya, who all live in Israel.

Visit Rabbi Kedar's website www.karynkedar.com, and follow her on Twitter (@kkedar) and Facebook.

CPSIA information can be obtained at www.ICGtesting.com
Printed in the USA
BVOW05s0050190314

348085BV00003B/27/P